KILMACURRAGH: SOURCED IN THE WILD

Kilmacurragh: sourced in the wild

The moulding of a heritage arboretum

Megan O'Beirne

SYSTEMS PUBLISHING

Text and photographs by Megan O'Beirne

First published in 2014 by Systems Publishing,
Villa Alba, Tara Hill, Gorey, Co. Wexford, Ireland.
Tel. +353 (0) 5394 22294;
www.systemspublishing.com

ISBN: 978-1905404-20-9 Paperback
ISBN: 978-1-905404-21-6 Hardback

This book was published with the assistance of Artlinks in
association with Wexford County Council.
Printed in Spain by Graficas Castuera

For my husband Patrick,
and in memory of my beloved parents, Marie and Michael Fleming

'Whenever man selects a place for a plant or a plant for a place, he is then in the domain of art, exercising the faculty of taste—taste an endowment of the human soul—taste which is so subjective and readily readable'[1]

TABLE OF CONTENTS

Foreword

I am delighted and honoured to have been invited by the author, Megan O'Beirne, to contribute a foreword for this splendid new book, highlighting a garden that is both very dear to me and one which could so easily have been lost. Today there are over 3,200 botanic gardens worldwide, a global network of gardens dedicated to botanical research, living collection management, horticultural excellence, environmental education and plant conservation. Ironically for a garden of such historical importance, Kilmacurragh is amongst a vanguard of new botanic gardens building on early origins to find contemporary roles and relevance for present-day Ireland. Megan O'Beirne is to be congratulated on bringing together so well the story of the garden, beautifully illustrated with hundreds of her excellent photographs, and helping to build an appreciation of Kilmacurragh for diverse new audiences and visitors. The story of Kilmacurragh is one that deserved to be told, where its heroes can be celebrated, from the Acton family founders right up to the present day, when its restoration has been achieved thanks to the vision of the Office of Public Works (OPW) and an army of dedicated staff of the National Botanic Gardens. The author has my admiration and thanks, that we can now enjoy the garden not only by visiting but also by reading her fine book.

My very first visit to Kilmacurragh was in 2005, shortly after my appointment as Director of the National Botanic Gardens in Glasnevin. I knew very little about the garden then, except that it had come through some desperately difficult times of neglect until its 'rescue' by the OPW in 1996 as a satellite garden for the National Botanic Gardens. This was acknowledged as probably its last hope for survival. Growing up as a teenager in County Wicklow, as a family we would often visit some of the other great gardens of the region, particularly Mount Usher and Powerscourt. I had never even heard of Kilmacurragh. When it was first brought under the care of the Glasnevin Gardens it was in a sorry state of neglect and dereliction. The great historic house, today a ruin and decaying fast, was badly damaged after a series of devastating fires (let us hope that one day it can be restored to become, once again, the heart of this great garden). What remained of the garden, now called 'Kilmacurragh Arboretum', was a shadow of its former glory. Anything other than woody plants had long since succumbed under acres and acres of weeds—brambles and laurels and much more besides.

In the 'new era' for Kilmacurragh, head gardener Paul Norton transferred down from Glasnevin to begin the 'rediscovery'. Slowly the secrets were revealed. After several years Paul returned to Glasnevin, many heroic tasks completed. Seamus O'Brien took his place and, together with his small, dedicated, energetic and enthusiastic team, continued the restoration. On every visit I made, Seamus would take justifiable pride in pointing out his latest discovery. One week it might be a lost rhododendron tree revealed from the undergrowth. His research would show that it had been grown from seed collected in the Himalayas by Sir Joseph Hooker of Kew in the 1840s or 1850s. On the next visit it might be a long-lost pathway, some buried steps or a trickling stream or ferny folly. Another time an old story might be told of the connections between the original owners, the Acton family, and their friends and collaborators at Glasnevin, most notably its former director, Sir Frederick Moore. A remarkable range of rare and sometimes unique specimens remained, collected by some of the world's greatest plant-hunters, their names almost a lexicon of those who created the suite of plants we grow in our temperate gardens today: Frank Kingdon-Ward, William Lobb, Joseph Hooker, E.H. Wilson, Augustine Henry, George Forrest—the list goes on.

As time went on, I became as excited about the garden and its history as Seamus and the team. Seamus would outline plans for ambitious replanting, not only showcasing the botanical treasures that survived but also enhancing them with plants either exchanged with colleagues at other great gardens, such as the Royal Botanic Garden, Edinburgh, or collected as seed by the current generation of staff from the National Botanic Gardens, from China, Chile, North America and the Himalayas in particular. I watched as new features were created or restored, such as the restored double borders, species-rich wildflower meadows, geographic plantings, native hedges and, most recently, the old entrance and its new avenue of monkey-puzzle tree (*Araucaria araucana*) plantings. When a small team of expert education staff was put in place and regular events held, open to the public, Kilmacurragh began at last to receive what it deserves: more and more visitors.

In the summer of 2010, it was a proud moment for all of us when hundreds of delegates from around the world attending the 4th Global Botanic Gardens Congress, hosted by the National Botanic Gardens in Glasnevin, travelled down for the day to visit Kilmacurragh. They came to see the garden and its collections, including many species that are rare or endangered in the wild that are being actively conserved at Kilmacurragh. In honour of the occasion, the Minister of State for the OPW, Dr Martin Mansergh, declared that Kilmacurragh Arboretum would henceforth become and be known as the 'National Botanic Gardens, Kilmacurragh'. It was truly recognition that Kilmacurragh was 'back on the map' and able to hold its head high amongst the great gardens of Ireland—and, indeed, of the world. A garden is never static; some of the 'champion' trees of Kilmacurragh will go, as they reach the end of their lives, but we can be cheered that today they will be replaced by worthy successors, ensuring that the garden will continue to be important and live on for future generations.

Often when I visited Kilmacurragh during my tenure at the National Botanic Gardens (2005–10) we would say, 'There are so many great stories to tell about Kilmacurragh—its history, its plants, the personalities amongst its owners, staff, collaborators and visitors, its dereliction and its restoration'. We would often repeat, 'Someone needs to write a book about it'. I am thrilled, therefore, that Megan O'Beirne has taken on this task and has created a book that is a delight to read, so full of the stories that will make this great garden come alive for visitors. Her book will help to make this garden better known, too. It is still undiscovered by far too many people in Ireland, many who hurry past on the nearby Dublin to Wexford N11 road, unaware that an oasis of history, biodiversity and heritage lies just a few miles to the west. This book will open the eyes of many to this national treasure.

Peter Wyse Jackson
President, Missouri Botanical Garden, St Louis
December 2014

Acknowledgements

My husband Patrick for his loving support and continual expert technical assistance.

The staff of theNational Botanic Gardens, Kilmacurragh, Kilbride, Co. Wicklow, who first stimulated my interest in the property by sharing their knowledge and kindly accompanying me on the walks in the early stages of my research. I wish to thank the Head Gardener, Seamus O'Brien, who first introduced me to the garden. I particularly wish to thank the guides Myles Reid, Philip Quested and Claire Mullarney for sharing their knowledge.

The Director and the following members of staff of the National Botanic Gardens, Glasnevin, Dublin: Matthew Jebb, Director, for his advice on certain particulars and for permission to quote from the 'Kilmacurragh Book' and to copy pages from Thomas Acton's Garden Diary; Paul Maher, Curator, National Botanic Gardens, Glasnevin, and National Botanic Gardens, Kilmacurragh, for his patient assistance with identification of plants; the Librarian, Alexandra Caccamo, and Library Assistant, Colette Edwards, for their generous professional assistance; Colin Kelleher, the Herbarium, for assistance with plant identification.

Dr David Thompson, Coillte Genetics and Tree Improvement Project, Kilmacurragh, Co. Wicklow.

Brian Donnelly, Archivist, and the staff of the National Archives, Bishop Street, Dublin.

Dr David Griffin, Director, and Library staff, Irish Architectural Archive, 45 Merrion Square, Dublin 2.

Turtle Bunbury, historian, for sharing his research on the Acton family with me.

Ken Hannigan, former Keeper of the National Archives, editor and historian, for his numerous professional recommendations and wonderfully generous assistance.

Jane Powers, garden writer and photographer, who generously shared her research on the subject with me.

Ciara Brennan, Librarian, Ballywaltrim Library, Bray, Co. Wicklow.

Gerard Whelan, Librarian, Royal Dublin Society, Ballsbridge, Dublin.

Staff of the Map Library, Trinity College, Dublin.

Office of Minister J. Deenihan, Department of Arts, Heritage and the Gaeltacht, Dáil Éireann.

Elizabeth Gilbert and the library staff, Royal Horticultural Society, Vincent Square, SW1, London.

The staff of the Library, Royal Botanic Garden, Edinburgh, for their assistance regarding the registration of 'Rhododendron Thomas Acton'.

The staff of the Library, Conservatory and Botanical Garden of the City of Geneva (Conservatoire et Jardin Botanique de la Ville de Genève), Chemin de l'impératrice 1, Chambesy 1292, Switzerland, for introducing me to relevant material.

Joan Kavanagh, historian, for her account of the research she undertook on behalf of Wicklow County Council, in the preparation of the exhibits in Wicklow's Historic Gaol.

Members of my family and numerous friends who were supportive of this project.

INTRODUCTION

Retreating to a garden full of trees on a day when ideas jostled and rain spilled, I caught the healing offered by a woodland environment. Odours were more intense, especially that of the eucalyptus trees, my feet crushing their leaves randomly strewn on the sodden woodland floor. The grace and harmony of a Japanese acer fixed my gaze. I discovered, too, that one doesn't walk alone among trees—they are powerful presences that have an enlarging effect on the heart. These giants of natural architecture spread their benign spirit, renew one's sense of purpose in the world, restore happiness, and even engender a sense of ecstasy. The concept of the tree as God's dwelling doesn't seem fanciful.

As I reviewed my photographs, companions to this text, especially those which close in with an almost myopic intensity, I realised my urge to 'scry' nature, to uncover the hidden the better to empathise, to capture form and textures, to plumb new depths for me of the very essence of the natural world. Having set out in Kilmacurragh arboretum with my enquiring lenses, I realise now that my work is as much exploratory as illustrative of a heritage demesne which reveals its many layers slowly, rewarding patience and presence. A single sturdy gatepost, kerbstones peeping through a grassy walkway, an abandoned driveway overgrown yet still discernible, the lie of a stand of trees—all trigger the imagination and help fill in those blanks where mere facts fall short.

I initially went to Kilmacurragh in 2009 in search of an exhibition site for photographs inspired by the ravages of the bark-beetle on the lodge-pole trees in Canada. I found instead a natural theatre with the remnants of a mansion, luxuriant vegetation and exotic tree collections recently wrested from the stranglehold of briar and laurel. Every twisted branch, angled trunk and grassed-over pathway spoke of a dramatic and complex history.

I was reminded of the words of the then head gardener, Paul Norton, in conversation with garden writer Jane Powers in April 1998, when he was single-handedly using mainly 'mattock, lopper and bushman's saw and spade' to rescue the gardens from the vice-like grip of bramble, holly, cherry, laurel and sycamore after decades of neglect:

> 'There are a lot of hidden things that people walk past without seeing. As I gradually get rid of the undergrowth you can actually *see*, the original layout of the garden becomes apparent, and you can *see* little vistas that you didn't know were there until you started to clear them.'[2]

Today we can only applaud his work and that of his successors in their efforts to reclaim this jewel of gardening history.

LEFT A dizzily leaning Hartweg's pine (*Pinus hartwegii*), with to its right the eucalyptus tree (*Eucalyptus pulverulenta*) that succumbed to the storms of February 2014. This eucalyptus tree is native to New South Wales and was brought to Europe in 1819. This tree was 35m tall.

As for me, another project was born—a resolution to fill a vacuum, to make an art-book comprising words and images which attempted to capture the spirit of the place as I experienced it. For me, a lay person in a specialist world to which, however, everyone has right of access, it was a tempting if audacious challenge. Over a span of four or five years (2009–14) changes occurred in the Arboretum and Gardens in accordance with the ongoing development of a special four-year management plan. This book, therefore, is a record of how things were during that period, a time of transition during which some old features were replaced, untidy corners were cleaned out and—alas—some of the oldest trees in the collection succumbed to the forces of nature.

BELOW A February perspective, with the 'needle point' of the oriental spruce (*Picea orientalis*) in the distance.

A dramatic arena

The most evocative symbol that captures the drama of the heritage property National Botanic Gardens, Kilmacurragh, in County Wicklow is that of an arena or theatre. The drama that unfolded there over the course of four centuries had a cast of seven generations of the Anglo-Irish Acton family. Each century presented scenes of contending opposites, from the humdrum aspects of running a farm, extending the reach of the demesne, planting amenity trees and playing a key role in local affairs to the most cataclysmic events in Irish history. The seventeenth century climaxed in the Rising of 1641, the eighteenth in the 1798 Rebellion, the nineteenth in a series of famines culminating in the Great Famine of 1846–50, and later the Land Acts (1870, 1881) which led to the eventual collapse of the landlord system in Ireland. The twentieth century was marked by the Great War (1914–18), which took a heavy toll on the Acton family and their staff and placed a financial burden on the property that led to its eventual sale in 1944.

These political events had a profound effect on the nation of Ireland, driving it towards an ineluctable political goal, while they affected the Anglo-Irish settler community in different ways. As the drama progressed over time, running themes jostled in a continuous struggle: wealth and misery, possession and dispossession, deforestation and silviculture, health and death, Protestant and Catholic, peace and aggression, power and impotence, occupancy and homelessness, hierarchical administration and democratic governance.

Today, the mute ruin of the mansion—a forgotten prop and a silent witness—still poignantly commands an elevated seaward view over the noble trees of the arboretum. The drama is spent, save for the seasonal raging storms, for which there is no repair.

BELOW Atlas cedar (*Cedrus atlantica*). The spreading branches of this large evergreen conifer welcome us into a mellow woodland garden in autumn.

ABOVE 'A mute ruin': the Queen Anne mansion that can
no longer speak for itself.

ABOVE The front lawn.
The contrasting habits of these two exotic trees
have made them iconic, and synonymous with
Kilmacurragh. The tall oriental spruce (*Picea
orientalis*), native to the Caucasus and eastern
Turkey, is over 100 years old and stands to a
height of over 30m. To its right is a Japanese red
cedar or cloud tree (*Cryptomeria japonica
'Elegans'*); a single tree, it is 30m across but only
6m high. This cultivar was introduced from Japan
by Thomas Lobb in 1854 and has distinctive
purple–red foliage in autumn.

ABOVE *Rhododendron arboreum* var. *cinnamomeum* (Joseph
Hooker).

Mexican cypress or cedar
of Goa (*Cupressus lusitanica
'Glauca Pendula'*).
One of the most attractive
conifers on the Glade.
Despite the reference to
Goa, this tree was first
introduced to Europe from
Mexico by Portuguese
missionaries in 1680. This
example is the height and
girth champion for Ireland
of this species.

1

THE NEW ORDER

Seven generations of Kilmacurragh's once-resident landowners, the Actons (an Anglo-Irish family, in Ireland since the 1640s), had a vision for their upland estate in Wicklow, a creative drive to fashion part of it into what ultimately became a world-acclaimed arboretum in the nineteenth century. The meticulous documentation they left behind tells of both their enthusiastic planting of amenity trees and their commercial interest in the timber industry. There are records also of their cooperation with various initiatives promoted by the Dublin Society (RDS) to replace woods that had been exploited to near extinction by both planters and natives over the previous centuries. During their continuous tenure (1697–1944) they planted a wide variety of both native and exotic trees of particular heritage and conservation interest to us today. Their collections include the ginkgo tree, 'a conifer with a fossil history going back 150 million years',[3] in the walled garden and varieties of equally ancient magnolias, as well as eighteenth- and nineteenth-century exotics sourced by intrepid plant-hunters. The prized conifer collection includes pines, spruces, silver firs, cedars, cypresses, hemlocks, redwoods, larch and hundreds of yews. The 'fluted' trunks and sprawling arms of the common yews (*Taxus baccata*)—some of them dating back to monastic times—embrace us from all sides, in particular in the Monk's Walk, where what was once a fashionable yew hedge is now overgrown and arches to form a sombre 'nave'. This is interrupted by the lily pond, a nineteenth-century replacement of two medieval fish-ponds used by the monks. The yews blend with naturalised deciduous trees such as the legendary sycamores and beeches, as well as with more recently introduced exotic conifer additions such as the towering Californian redwoods (*Sequoiadendron giganteum*). The dark foliage of the evergreens provides a dramatic backdrop to the precious Hooker tree-rhododendrons, widely acknowledged as the most beautiful woody flowering plants in the world. Hunted in the Himalayas by (Sir) Joseph Hooker in the 1800s, they were successfully nurtured by Thomas Acton (1826–1908).

The Actons left us a magnificent arboreal heritage. Their era is long over, and a new social order prevails. Their impact on the landscape, however, stands as a testimony to their vision and continues to be an inspiration to those currently restoring and developing the arboretum and gardens on behalf of the Irish state.

LEFT A giant sequoia or Sierra redwood (*Sequoiadendron giganteum*), one of the world's biggest trees, rises spire-like over the other exotic conifers on the Glade, which drops down to the pond.
In-house garden notes reveal that this giant sequoia was raised from William Lobb's collections in the Yosemite Valley, California.

'A sister garden'

In 1996 the Office of Public Works (OPW), on behalf of the government, entrusted the management of Kilmacurragh Arboretum and Gardens to the National Botanic Gardens (NBG), Glasnevin, Dublin, of which it is now 'a sister garden'. Today the historical, carefully tended tree collections are interplanted with more recently acquired wild-sourced rarities collected during expeditions organised by the NBG to South Africa, central China, Taiwan, Belize, Siberia and South America. The 2002 Central China Expedition was led by the current head gardener at Kilmacurragh, Seamus O'Brien. Plant acquisitions made during such expeditions have enabled a new style of gardening in which specially designated phyto-geographical zones, i.e. representative of specific countries, are created. Those relating to China and Chile are outstanding examples of this style. In addition, the arboretum now has a growing seed bank, a herbarium, and conservation and education programmes, all of which guarantee the continuing importance of Kilmacurragh in both botanical and conservation terms in Ireland and globally.

TOP LEFT The strictly erect trunk of the giant sequoia is covered with fibrous cinnamon-brown bark, which breaks off in irregular, thickish plates and insulates the tree during forest fires.

TOP RIGHT Exotic conifers reflected in the lily pond.

RIGHT Detail of *Photinia villosa* var. *sinica*, China.

OPPOSITE PAGE An enormous willow-leaved podocarp (*Podocarpus salignus*), sourced in Chile by William Lobb in 1850, viewed from the Double Borders.
'The young plants of this willow-leaved podocarp in the arboretum are all seedlings from this big tree.' [4]

Some champion trees

Until February 2014, six of Kilmacurragh's many heritage trees which were originally brought to Europe by nineteenth-century plant-hunters from far-off temperate zones were champions by virtue of their height and girth. In the fierce storms that raged in that month two of these prized champions were lost, namely the Patagonian cypress (*Fitzroya cupressoides*) and the powdered gum or silver-leaved mountain gum (*Eucalyptus pulverulenta*). Both species are termed vulnerable and on the Red Data list, meaning that they are threatened with extinction in their countries of origin. Like many of the original wild-sourced trees in Kilmacurragh, both lost trees had been propagated or cloned using the most recent techniques, in order to have replacements for them in due course and to reintroduce them to their places of origin if necessary. Some of these are already *in situ*, including young specimens of the willow-leaved podocarp, *Podocarpus salignus*—all raised from seedlings from the magnificent big tree near the car park. The young monkey-puzzle trees newly planted in the old avenue are a mixture of self-sown seedlings from the old avenue and plants donated by the Royal Botanic Garden, Edinburgh[5]—surely a promise and a guarantee for the future.

TOP RIGHT 'The young plants of the willow-leaved podocarp in the arboretum are all seedlings from the big tree above.'

MIDDLE RIGHT Young Chile pine or monkey-puzzle tree (*Araucaria araucana*), exotic among the simple spring flowers.

BOTTOM RIGHT The logged remains of the treasured Patagonian cypress (*Fitzroya cupressoides*) from Chile, blown down during the storm. Plans are afoot to have the colourful wood preserved in sculpture form.
This photograph was taken in February 2014 after the worst storm in the history of Ireland. Happily, the tree has been successfully propagated, as young saplings in the arboretum testify.

The gardens and arboretum—a general profile

The National Botanic Gardens, Kilmacurragh, Kilbride, Co. Wicklow, are about an hour and fifteen minutes' drive, travelling southwards from Dublin via the N11.[6] If their existence is a well-kept secret, it could have something to do with the very discreet heritage sign on the N11, which reads 'Kilmacurra' (a reference to the townlands adjacent to the arboretum), with no textual reference to the Botanical Gardens and Arboretum. One suspects that this omission contributes to the welcome, if slightly selfish, benefit that the arboretum, while well known to local families and in botanical circles, is never inundated with unmanageable

TOP LEFT Patagonian cypress (*Fitzroya cupressoides*), one of the champion trees lost in the violent storm of February 2014.

TOP RIGHT A close view of the powdered gum or silver-leaved mountain gum (*Eucalyptus pulverulenta*).
This wonderful old champion tree was blown down during the violent storms of February 2014.

numbers of visitors, thus ensuring a tranquil visit.

Since 1944, when the arboretum and gardens were sold by Charles Acton, the last heir in residence, the garden has had periods of troughs— some have said 'blessed neglect'—when it reverted to a semi-wild state. Unfortunately, the steady decline of the mansion in that period means that now it is merely a secured ruin, a natural roost for crows.

Happily, since 1996, after almost 50 years of various lessees and owners, the arboretum and gardens are under secure management and now have the status of Botanical Gardens, referred to as the 'country estate' of the National Botanic Gardens, Glasnevin, Dublin. As well as the head gardener, there are, as I write, two sub-gardeners and three other staff members, who provide the excellent garden guide service during the summer.

The area of the arboretum and gardens accessible to the public comprises 52 acres, a fraction of the once 6,000-acre demesne. This compares favourably, however, with the accessible areas of other County Wicklow demesnes open to the public: Powerscourt (45 acres, excluding the waterfall area), nearby Mount Usher (22 acres) and the more comparable Altamont, Tullow, Co. Carlow (40 acres). The garden is luckily girdled by another 50 acres of forestry trees, including an area, once the Deer Park, where nursery trees are now grown as part of a Coillte commercial research project managed by the Forestry Department of the Office of Public Works. This insulating green belt and the surrounding working farms are an ideal backdrop and contribute to the sense of privacy and tranquillity in the gardens.

Kilmacurragh and other contemporary Irish demesnes were principally owned by the Anglo-Irish, the Ascendancy landlord class, some of them English gentlemen of Irish birth and extremely loyal to Britain. They tended to mirror the gardening styles exemplified in contemporary English properties of similar size. The focal point

was a mansion of architectural merit of variable size, surrounded by formal gardens planted with an ornate and often exotic mix of deciduous and coniferous trees. There were water features such as ponds or lakes or even canals (as in early eighteenth-century Kilmacurragh), statuary, a well-stocked deer park and a nursery for private propagation, all of which was often ringed by an informal pastoral landscape including the family farm, and wooded shelter-belts usually of lime, sycamore and other 'native' species. In addition, in Ireland the mansion was often built on the site of a castle or, as was the case in Kilmacurragh, on the ruins of a monastery.

As well as the fascination of a beautiful, historical garden, with its valuable tree collections, and easy access from the N11, there is the added attraction of the human scale of the 52-acre property, which means that the garden can be walked in a leisurely hour or so. The well-maintained, user-friendly paths, ample parking and toilet facilities make the arboretum and gardens an exceptional recreational venue for families, the elderly, artists and photographers. At the time of writing, some of the outhouses are being reconstructed for the welcome provision of a cafeteria, while the many picnic tables offer alternative arrangements so popular with visitors.

Kilmacurra–Westaston–Kilmacurragh

The place-name 'Kilmacurragh' evolved from the foundation of a medieval church there, named after St Mochorog. There are different forms of the name dating from the thirteenth century ('Kilmechur'), the sixteenth century ('Kilmethur') and 1655 ('Kilmachurra'), variants referenced in Chapter 2. A document dated 1729 in the Ainsworth report on the Acton papers in the National Library, Dublin, refers to the Acton demesne as 'the lands of Kilmacurra'. Kilmacurra

is actually the name of the two townlands to the north and east of Kilmacurragh, which itself sits in the townland of Westaston Demesne, as Matthew Jebb, Director of the NBG, informed me. This explains why the estate referred to as 'Kilmacurragh' in the 1817 lease document was later named Westaston Demesne. Westaston Hill, once part of the property, is now in private ownership. In the mid-nineteenth century the name of the estate reverted to 'Kilmacurragh', the Anglicised spelling being that used by Petty's surveyors of the lands in the seventeenth century and since perpetuated. It was the Acton family seat for seven generations, spanning almost 300 years, from 1697 to 1944. Their original leasing and continuous tenure of the lands and the gradual evolution of the gardens occurred against a backdrop of some of the most dramatic episodes of Irish political and social history, as already specified.

ABOVE An insulating green belt on Westaston Hill.

A sense of melancholy

The slightly melancholic atmosphere of the old place is conjured by the very stones of the spectral mansion (thriftily salvaged from the ruins of the monastery), by the pond-side cairn surmounting the bones of the exhumed remains of monks and by the old wind-tried trees, each with its unique history of acquisition. Centuries-old yews, ancient oaks and ash trees, huge specimens of Himalayan and western North American hemlocks and Chinese firs stand tall or lean along the old paths which dip down into the woody middle distance. There a segment of the old Coach Road with its march of ancient oaks, dubbed the 'dark lane' in the past, is now known as the Oak Avenue. The

ABOVE LEFT 'and each particular trunk a growth / Of intertwisted fibres serpentine upcoiling' (Wordsworth, 'Yew Trees').

TOP Skeletal branches of yew trees (*Taxus baccata*).

ABOVE A contorted *Rhododendron 'altaclerense'* near the Double Borders tells its own story of survival before the rescue operation in the gardens took place in 1998.

contorted limbs of old rhododendrons, including precious specimens of the Hooker collection such as *Rhododendron fortunei*, *R. griffithianum* and the many specimens of *R. arboreum*, are sculpted by time into nature's filigree. Silent witnesses, too, are the *faux* Gothic arch, the wrought-iron gates, the stone stile, remnants of the old summerhouse and the occasional 'blind' signpost. Surviving descriptive names echo the daily activities on the estate down the generations: 'the turnip field', 'the bleaching field', 'the 'Clash field', 'the horses' graveyard', the Deer Park with its surrounding ha-ha, 'the Monk's Walk', 'the shady lane', the walled stable-yard, the Victorian Double Borders and the Broad Walk.

Not a mere reliquary

Yet Kilmacurragh is not just a place of exhumed bones and evocative names; it also has a dynamic present. It is cared for to a high professional standard and there is an air of progressive planting, especially in the Chinese and South American sections and in an imaginative remodelling of tired features. A case in point is the impressive, newly laid (spring 2013) replacement hedge of mixed native shrubs which makes an old boundary to the right of the driveway sing. The sheer variety of shrubs in the hedge symbolise for me all that is vital and exciting about the arboretum today. They include hazel, ash, oak, holly, blackthorn, hawthorn, crab-apple, strawberry tree, spindle bush and guelder rose.[7] The many young specimen trees and

OPPOSITE PAGE, CLOCKWISE FROM TOP LEFT
The eighteenth-century gate leading into the Deer Park.

One of those intriguing 'blind' signposts. Myles Reid, one of the guides, first drew my attention to this curious relic.

The stone stile giving access from the Oak Avenue to the Barndarrig–Rathdrum road.

A nineteenth-century nod to a monastic past.

ABOVE RIGHT The derelict summerhouse, ivy-draped.

shrubs punctuating the glades, the fruits of recent expeditions, secure the inheritance for future generations. This skilful juxtaposition of the old and the new illustrates natural cycles and the slow progression of time and represents a secure investment in the future of this elegant Arboretum and National Botanical Gardens.

A hospitable garden

The secret of Kilmacurragh's success as a famous garden dating from the eighteenth century rests primarily in its humus-rich soil and its micro-climate of high rainfall. It offered what the famous English botanist W.T. Thistleton-Dyer[8] referred to as 'hospitality to exotic vegetation' in his writings about these islands, the then British Isles, at the turn of the nineteenth century.

Undoubtedly, the success of the arboretum is predicated on its fundamental wealth, comprising its soil, situation and orientation. These factors received special mention in the 1931 Report of the Royal Horticultural Society, London, on the occasion of the awarding of the Banks Medal to Thomas Acton (1826–1908) for his outstanding collection of conifers. Distinguishing factors which facilitated the growth of tender species in Kilmacurragh were listed: its 'high altitude near the sea', its 'Northerly aspect' and 'the form of the ground', which 'reduces the possibility of frost damage'. Further, the Report continues, 'It is well sheltered from the prevailing South-west wind both by rising ground and by tall trees on the windward side'. The soil type was described as 'a deep fresh loam' which is of 'an open porous nature' on higher ground, while 'the lower parts are damp and firm in texture, and is free from all traces of lime'.[9]

Botanical Gardens, brought their calcifuge or lime-hating plants and ones of 'doubtful hardiness' to Kilmacurragh, where conditions were ideal, unlike the limy and cold conditions at Glasnevin, which were totally unsuitable for them. After having been established in the acidic humus of Kilmacurragh, the clones of these rhododendrons were sent to Glasnevin and elsewhere, where, in Charles Acton's words, they 'populated many of the fine collections of Ireland'.

Acton drew a distinction between the colourful display of the common species, the cultivar rhododendron '*altaclerense*', in the Broad Walk, which Whaley found so striking, and the real glory of Kilmacurragh, namely the other species of rhododendrons sourced in the wild by (Sir) Joseph Hooker, including *R. falconeri*, *R. loderi*, *R. thomsonii*, *R. barbatum*, *R. shepherdii* and others.

ABOVE *Rhododendron grande*, blossom detail, a specimen from the 1849 Hooker collection originally raised in Glasnevin and then successfully trialled by Thomas Acton.

The 'essence of the collection'—the Moore connection

Who is more entitled to convey the importance of Kilmacurragh than the late Charles Acton (1914–1999), well-known music critic and the last member of the Acton family to own the demesne which he sold in 1944? In response to an article in the *Irish Times*[11] written by their correspondent Jack Whaley (28 April 1984), Acton was at pains to explain the 'essence of the collection' at Kilmacurragh. Central to the importance of the rhododendron collection at Kilmacurragh, he explained, was the fact that exotic plants sourced in the wild were deposited in both Kew Gardens, London, and the Botanic Gardens, Glasnevin. David Moore and his son Frederick (the latter affectionately known in the Acton household as 'Sir Freddie'), successive curators of the Royal

The arboretum and gardens—a preview

This in-house map (right) is a guide to the different areas in the arboretum and gardens. Specific areas included, in clockwise order, are the Fossil Plant Lawn, the Native Wildflower Meadow, the Chinese Plants, the Sino-Himalayan Plants, the Pond and the Monk's Walk. The Oak Avenue, unmarked, is south of the Yew Avenue. Next are the Himalayan Plants, Temperate South American Plants, the Broad Walk or the Rhododendron and Yew Avenue, and the Double Borders. A small lawn planted with some of the oldest trees in the arboretum lies between the Broad Walk and the Double Borders, both at the back of the mansion.

Modest granite pillars mark the current official entrance to the arboretum. The narrow, serpentine avenue, recently upgraded, which was developed by Coillte[12] during their early tenure, curves through parkland, with occasional single 'parking bays' to ease traffic flow. This avenue is punctuated by a stand of silver birch, some randomly planted mixed forestry trees such as Sitka spruce, Scots pine and birch, as well as Atlantic cedars and tree-

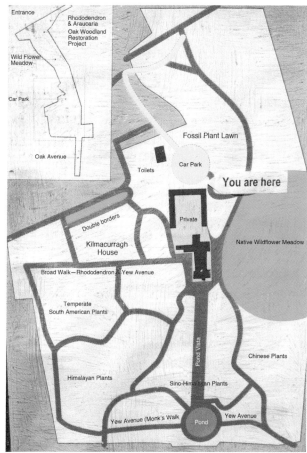

ABOVE In-house map of the gardens and arboretum. Courtesy of NBG Glasnevin.

rhododendrons, with occasional specimen oak and beech trees, all enhanced by magical tangled coppices. Before the modern development of the arboretum and gardens, one of the Educational Guides, Myles Reid, explained that this avenue was possibly a meandering path of convenience for the estate workers, many of whom lived in the adjacent demesne village of Kilcandra. Hearsay has it that a shebeen close to the entrance was a tempting distraction for some of the workers, who had to be summoned to prayers by a loud-clanging bell! Through convenience and usage, the driveway has replaced the now-closed original carriageway, which was planted with double-sided silver firs and monkey-puzzles and has recently been restocked as part of the woodland renewal plan. It will become the main entrance again, according to the plans. Geometrically straight, it intersects the closed road which once skirted the estate, and traces suggest that it then curved fashionably to the gravelled sweep in front of the mansion.

OPPOSITE PAGE, CLOCKWISE FROM TOP LEFT
Early buds of the tree-peony (*Paeonia lutea*)
which captures our attention just inside the
wooden gate into the garden proper.

Summer blossoms of the tree-peony (*Paeonia lutea*).

Autumn seed-pods of the tree-peony (*Paeonia lutea*) spill open.

Autumn leaf of tree-peony (*Paeonia lutea*).

BELOW Out-of-bounds secured relic of the mansion.

BELOW RIGHT Ginkgos, maidenhair tree.
Seven-year-old seedlings raised from the ancient
giants at Bai Sha were planted out into their
permanent positions on the Fossil Lawn at
Kilmacurragh in 2009.

A wildflower meadow set out in experimental patchwork sections (2009–13) once scrolled to the left as one proceeded along the avenue and into the arboretum car park, located in the newly landscaped eighteenth-century stable-yard. At one point the avenue, flanked by handsome evergreen and deciduous trees, branches off to the right, leading to the Coillte Tree Research Centre located in the walled garden. Passing from the car park through the gate by the notice-board, a panorama opens out to the east, with a sliver of Wicklow Bay discernible on a fine day. Commanding the eastern view stands the out-of-bounds secured relic of the eighteenth-century mansion, built on the site of a medieval monastery church that was sacked in the thirteenth century.

The orientation of the mansion naturally determined the layout of the gardens in the 1700s. Reconstructed according to its original design, the mansion could conceivably be a vibrant focal point once again. To date, however, the unequivocal remit of the current management has been solely the restoration of the arboretum and its plant collections, and they discharge their responsibility with outstanding dedication and flair. The future of the mansion is of course subject to change with time.

Standing on the gravelled 'sweep' in front of the house, looking eastwards, the eye traces the contours of Collon (Cullen) Hill, the pastoral landscape of the surrounding farmland and the closer lawn—a sea of native wildflowers in summer and of wild crocuses in spring.

To the east lies the 'Fossil Lawn', where the relatively recent planting of gymnosperm trees such as the ginkgos transport us to the Jurassic era,

ABOVE One of several of the fossil species dawn redwoods (Metasequoia) in the Fossil Lawn (Sichuan–Hubei region of China).

when dinosaurs browsed on their soft foliage. 'The ginkgo is a conifer with a fossil history going back 190 million years, making it the longest extant genus of plant known.'[13] The four seven-year-old ginkgos (*Ginkgo biloba*) planted in 2009 in the Fossil Lawn were removed for emergency care in 2013. They were grown 'from the seeds of fruits picked from old trees at the little village of Bai Sha in Badong County, high above the Three Gorges, in Central China'.[14] It is unlikely, however, given local conditions, that these slow-growing ten-year-olds will live for thousands of years like those

festooned specimens in Buddhist temples in Japan. In Kilmacurragh in 2012 they were well spaced, protected and mulched where they grew alongside other living fossils such as Wollemi pines, monkey-puzzles and dawn redwoods. We look forward to their reintroduction.

The well-trodden path dips along the natural contours of the land among centuries-old chestnut and oak trees and nineteenth-century plantings of rare rhododendrons such as Joseph Hooker's *Rhododendron falconeri* and towering specimen trees like Hartweg's pine, native to Mexico and Central

ABOVE Monk's Walk—a 'nave' of common yews (*Taxus baccata*).

ABOVE Water lilies, *Nymphaea alba*.

OPPOSITE PAGE Wind-tossed oaks in the 'Oak Avenue', part of the old Coach Road closed in 1818.

LEFT *Rhododendron 'altaclerense'* self-seedling nods towards the Chinese fir (*Cunninghamia lanceolata* 'Glauca') near the lily pond.

OPPOSITE PAGE *R. 'altaclerense'* on the Broad Walk: 'A decorative display of a common species' (Charles Acton).

RIGHT Japanese (Hinoki) cypress (*Chamaecyparis obtusa*).

LEFT *Rhododendron grande* (Hooker).

LEFT King Billy's Pine (*Athrotaxis selaginoides*) (Tasmania). This tree is rated as 'Vulnerable' in Tasmania in the Red Data List. This specimen is the Irish champion for height (25m) and girth (2.5m)—measurements recorded in the tree trail notes on compilation.

America, and the subtropical powdered gum from Australia.[15] The Chinese Garden lies to the east, with lots of rare additions from recent expeditions, including some Chinese gooseberries, *Actinidia chinensis*, also sourced in the Three Gorges region of central China.

A line of old oak trees along the present boundary draws the eye and guides our feet into a section of the long-closed old Coach Road, now known as 'the Oak Avenue'. Here a splendid double row of hybrid oaks with wide-spreading crowns display the occasional limb whipped bare by the east wind. This avenue in particular is a vivid indicator of the passing seasons, as gaunt winter boles crisp into spring freshness, changing to leafy summer foliage and finally to autumn glory. A stone stile at the top of the incline gives access to the Rathdrum road. The garden guides proudly describe it as 'one of the finest oak stands in Ireland' and often link it, perhaps fancifully, to Cromwell's notorious route from Rathdrum to Wexford. This was also the route taken by carts conveying Avoca ore and ore from the Conary mines to the nearby ports of Wicklow and Arklow. In a letter to archivist and historian Ken Hannigan, the late Charles Acton wrote that 'the 'Clash field' had an old shaft in it where iron was mined, and 'the ore was smelted there with oak brought from Ballinaclash and the resulting pigiron was then taken to Arklow for export'.[16] Veering westward, a natural yew 'tunnel' now arches over the 'Monk's Walk'—anecdotally an old pilgrims' path to Glendalough. This dark nave is bisected by the lily pond, which is fed by a streamlet.

TOP RIGHT The exotic Chinese/Japanese banana (*Musa basjoo*), Double Borders.

BOTTOM RIGHT Chinese/Japanese banana (*Musa basjoo*) swaddled in its protective winter casing in the Double Borders.

Towering clumps of Himalayan tree-rhododendrons—all sourced in the wild—as well as the more showy hybrids *R. 'altaclerense'* make occasional secluded garden compartments. With the champion aromatic Chilean laurel to our left, we pass two giants, the Irish champion Himalayan hemlock and the western North American hemlock, and further along the *Rhododendron grande*, a specimen from the 1849 Hooker collection originally raised in Glasnevin and then successfully trialled by Thomas Acton. A grove of tall trees to the right, including an extraordinary golden hinoki (*Chamaeoparis obtusa Crippsii*), an impressive Mexican cypress (*Cupressus lusitanica*), a tiger-tail spruce and a Chinese mahogany (*Toona sinensis*), are grouped around the Tasmanian King William pine (*Athrotaxis selaginoides*)—one of the champion trees for height and girth in Kilmacurragh.

Our overview brings us to two seasonally colourful show-pieces of the garden, namely the Victorian Broad Walk and the stepped, floral Double Borders flanked by the Walled Garden, now headquarters of the Coillte research team and their trialling polytunnels.

Separating these two Victorian show-pieces is a lawn planted with exotics hunted in the 1800s, including the Japanese hiba with all of its fourteen stems, together with some of the oldest trees in the arboretum, such as the *Fraxinus excelsior* of European origin, the manna ash (*Fraxinus ornus*), Kilmacurragh's own Japanese red cedars and an enormous willow-leaved podocarp *(Podocarpus salignus)* hunted by William Lobb, my own favourite in the collection. Over the west wall of the Walled Garden towers the exquisitely beautiful pink *Magnolia campbellii*. Magnolias rank among the most ancient flowering plants. Joseph Hooker found this species outside Darjeeling in 1848.

The car park is but a few steps away, bringing us full circle.

ABOVE The loose and papery bark of the fuchsia tree (*Fuchsia excorticata*) near the Double Borders.

OPPOSITE PAGE Warm tints of crocosmia in the stepped Double Borders.
'The long, narrow slip of an enclosed flower garden is one of the most delightful and old-time like I ever saw.'[17] The wall encloses what was once the 'Monks' Orchard' and is now known as the Walled Garden. It is the site of Coillte tree-breeding experimentation.

RIGHT *Fascicularia bicolour* ssp. *bicolor* in the recently developed South American zone.

ABOVE *Magnolia campbellii.*
Planted in the Walled Garden, its brilliant pink blossoms overhang the still-
dormant Double Borders in March. This magnificent species is native to the
Himalayas from Nepal to Assam. Joseph Hooker found this species outside
Darjeeling in 1848.

An alternative starting point lies on the south side of the mansion and takes us down a broad grassy glade, bordered by some of the largest heritage trees in the arboretum, including specimen giant Californian redwoods, Japanese red cedars, podocarps and monkey-puzzle trees. The glade dips down to the pond and joins paths weaving through clusters of native yews, some of them hundreds of years old, and towering exotic trees from temperate climates. Following the purling watercourse, an intersection to the right is the South American zone, dedicated to a new ensemble of plants including the exotic Chilean *Fascicularia bicolor* ssp. *canaliculata.*

2

KILMACURRAGH— A SACRED SITE

A saint's hermitage—
a thirteenth-century church —
a graveyard

Previous page In a monastery garden.

Above left An ancient yew (*Taxus baccata*) near vestiges of an eighteenth-century wall.

Above Gushing waters flow through the estate from a reservoir on Westaston Hill.
They fill the lily pond and flow out into the Potter's River, which ultimately joins the Irish Sea at Brittas Bay.

Left Hong Kong lily (*Lilium brownii*), native to China.

ABOVE *Chamerion angustifolium* 'Album'.

ABOVE Close-up of the cairn marking the burial of the exhumed bones from the monks' graveyard.

RIGHT Thistle seed-head.

OPPOSITE PAGE, CLOCKWISE FROM TOP LEFT
Chinese rhubarb, *Rheum palmatum* 'Bowles
Crimson'.

Chinese rhubarb, *Rheum palmatum* 'Bowles
Crimson'

Gunnera—a poolside plant.

Chinese rhubarb, *Rheum palmatum* 'Bowles
Crimson'.

A sacred burial place—a monastic heritage

We know that Kilmacurragh has been associated with human burials from prehistoric to modern times. Early maps confirm this. Today the garden, with its distinctive, undulating contours, reflects its long history, from Neolithic times (fourth millennium BC) to the more immediate pre-Acton period, when it was in native Irish ownership (the O'Byrnes) and had a monastic settlement.

An unmistakable air of both the sacred and the melancholy clings to the very boughs of the hundreds of those primitive conifers, the common yew trees, in Kilmacurragh. Yews have always been symbols of longevity and transcendence and therefore their presence in what was once a monastery garden and graveyard is to be expected. Since Christian times yews have been planted in

BELOW 'Venerable yews of almost hoary antiquity'—Wordsworth.

churchyards and near priories and abbeys because of their sombre character, dark foliage and longevity. Paradoxically, they evoke simultaneously hope in the transcendent, a deep sense of veneration and sorrow at the inescapable reality of death.

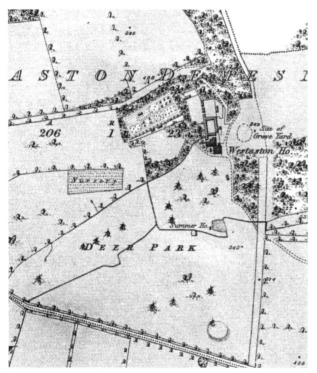

Historic monuments

The detail of the 1838 OS map of Westaston Demesne (Kilmacurragh) shown above indicates the presence of both pre-Christian and Christian monuments on its lands. The pre-Christian or Celtic fortified settlement, in the form of a rath dating probably from the Iron Age or early medieval times, was sited in the area south of the house later known as the Deer Park (now part of Coillte's tree research plantation). This rath had 'some graves in it', uncovered during the levelling operations carried out by Colonel William Acton in 1836.[18] The map also records the 'Site of Grave Yard'—the monks' graveyard, to the east of the mansion. This was also levelled at the same time for the purpose of laying a tennis court. The exhumed bones of the monks were placed under a cairn of loose stones, now mossy with age, near the lily pond. Removal of such monuments even to make way for more modern usage of the land would be unthinkable and, indeed, illegal in our time. Acton family folklore tells that the ruined monastery provided some of the building materials for their mansion, built between 1697 and 1716. There were many precedents for this practice in England and Wales. Apart from the thrift angle, the recycling of these materials established—unconsciously, perhaps—a link with the past and a profound, if imperceptible, awareness of the sacred connection.

The Acton mansion is believed to have been built on the actual site of the church; this is confirmed by Eugene O'Curry's Ordnance Survey Letter of 26 January 1839, which states that 'the probable site of Kilmachurra [sic] Church was at the door of Colonel Acton's house'.[19]

Christianity came to Ireland with the arrival of St Patrick in 432. His teaching eventually gave rise to many monastic settlements, one of the most important being that founded by St Kevin (498–618) in Glendalough, Co. Wicklow. As the Rt Revd R.W. Heavener writes, this monastery became 'the parent of several others' to which St Kevin assigned his followers, one of whom was St Mochorog of Delgany, after whose church the townland of Kilmacurra, Co. Wicklow, was named.[20] 'Kilmacurra' literally means the church (cill, the Gaelic word for church, Anglicised as 'kill') of Mochorog. In 1275 Kilmacurragh was known

as 'Kilmechur' and in 1531 as 'Kilmethur'. St Mochorog was by birth a Briton—he and his nine brothers were the sons of Diona, daughter of a king of the Saxons, and Brachan, king of the Britons (or Welsh).[21] The origins of his contemporary St Kevin were noble too, as *his* father 'sprang from the royal race of Leinster kings'. Local historian Ken Hannigan relates that local tradition places St Kevin's birthplace in Dunganstown and suggests that he received his training in the monastery at Kilnamanagh, not far from Kilmacurragh.

The saint is, however, listed as Mogoroc in the early lists of saints and as having been located in Delgany, in the barony of Rathdown, Co. Wicklow. Like his fellow contemplative, St Kevin of Glendalough, who shunned society for deserted places, we picture Mochorog having those qualities which Canon O'Hanlon attributes to St Kevin, namely 'greatness of soul' and 'force of character',[22] prompting him to withdraw from his monastery in Delgany to a cell in the remote woodlands of Kilmacurra. St Mochorog's cell, dating from the seventh century, probably evolved into a monastic settlement,[23] with its own church, graveyard, 'Chapel Orchard' and two ponds, which feature in the George Clanchy estate map of 1708. Liam Price confirms that 'there was a church (ecclesia) here in the thirteenth century', one of many in the

neighbourhood. Mochorog apparently had an intimate spiritual relationship with the saintly Abbot Kevin of Glendalough, to whom he was called to administer the last rites of the Church when he died in 618 at the great age of 120. With such evidence of a monastic settlement, imaginings are inevitable of prayerful meditation and the chanting of the Divine Office in the monastery chapel at Kilmacurragh.

Peace was short-lived, however. Historical facts tell of two centuries of violent looting of Irish monasteries by Viking hordes from Norway from 800 onward, to be followed in 1169 by waves of Norman, Welsh and Fleming knights recruited by Diarmuid Mac Morrough with the aim of recovering his kingdom in Leinster. They soon controlled the east coast and penetrated deep into the hinterland too; as Price records, 'by the year 1180 there were settlements by Normans, English and Welsh in almost all of Co. Wicklow'.

In 1275, some 650 years after St Mochorog's time, we learn that the rector of the Kilmacurra monastery, possibly its last, was John Albo Monestrerio, who died in that year 'on account of war', an ominous signal for the destruction of the monastery. Henry II had come to Ireland in 1171 and demanded the submission of the diocese of Dublin and Glendalough. Glendalough ceased to be a centre of learning in 1214, on the death of St Laurence O'Toole. Heavener recounts that the bishopric of Glendalough was significantly granted to an English appointee, John Comyn, in 1214, an example of the Anglicisation policy in Ireland. The final destruction of the monastery there, however, culminated in assassinations and ruin around the fourteenth century. Kilmacurra most probably met a similar fate at about the same time.

Anecdotally, St Mochorog, like St Kevin, had miraculous powers, illustrated by his capacity to 'bring his well with him' wherever he decided to settle—monks usually had ponds stocked with fish for the table. The ponds attracted herons, who, we are told in the nineteenth-century 'Kilmacurragh Book', often dropped the fish they had caught at sea on their return to their roost at Kilmacurragh, thus providing the family table with a handy meal! In 1889 Thomas Acton replaced these ponds with the present lily pond.

These features, remnants of the monastic church and graveyard, orchards and fish-ponds, are tangible reminders of the sacred nature of these lands.

Recent history

The tragic aspects of Acton family history contribute to the air of melancholy in the garden. There were the premature deaths of three of Col. William Acton's children, who died within a space of seven years (1834–41), and then the fatal traffic accident of William's nephew, Thomas Acton (1818–43), in the vicinity.

In his will, Thomas Acton (1826–1908), the most celebrated moulder of the arboretum, specified that he wished to be buried in the Deer Park near to *Pinus ponderosa*, one of his favourite trees, where his sister Janet had already been buried in 1906. (Formerly members of the Acton family had been buried in Rathdrum, and later in St

TOP LEFT Like a standard-bearer beside the Monk's Walk, this venerable yew is believed to be c. 500 years old. Possibly the oldest tree in the garden, it is credibly a living witness to monastic times and a symbol of a hallowed history. A clump of mistletoe atop a tree near the pond may hint at the existence of an earlier druidic sacred site here also.

BELOW LEFT A secluded cloister of common yews (*Taxus baccata*).
The fluted trunks and sprawling arms of numerous common yews are an arresting feature of the garden. They embrace us from all sides, in particular on the Monk's Walk. Once a fashionable yew hedge, planted in the 1820s by Col. William Acton, the overgrown trees now arch into a nave-like 'tunnel'. It is sometimes claimed that it bordered an early pilgrims' path leading to the monastery at Glendalough. The Monk's Walk is divided by the nineteenth-century lily pond, which replaced two of the original monks' fish-ponds.

LEFT The Acton tomb, the graveyard, St Kevin's Church of Ireland church, Dunganstown, Co. Wicklow.
Successive members of the Acton family were practising Christians closely associated with the Reformed Church of St Kevin in Dunganstown. Revd Thomas Acton (1792–1846) was rector there and is buried in the family tomb.

Kevin's Churchyard, Dunganstown, Co. Wicklow.) His wishes were carried out and, with time, nature has discreetly veiled their resting place from curious eyes.

Other material features in the arboretum are associated with painful historical episodes. The construction of the ha–ha, the sunken wall built to restrain the deer in the Deer Park, was a famine relief project in 1848, when starving workers from the west of Ireland were engaged to rebuild it. The prevailing questionable ethic of landlords organising the relief works—namely that earned money was preferable to charity—prompts one to question the physical condition of those men engaged in that work. Tales of a 'hanging tree' on the property, used during the rebellion of 1798, and the sighting of ghosts in the old mansion (!) compound the lugubrious undertow.

A lugubrious undertow

Ken Hannigan[24] recounts how John Francis Byrne, who during his childhood and early manhood spent his summers in the area and later wrote about them, remembered hearing about the 'fear the locals had of the supernatural' and how Byrne personally had heard three shrieks coming from near the Kilcandra entrance to the Acton estate. The local priest, Fr Moloney, had the frightening experience while making a sick call by way of the 'Dark Lane' from Barndarrig to Rathdrum of having his coach, coachman and horse 'lifted off the road and deposited in Colonel's Acton's deer

park at a point where there was no possible route of access for a horse and car'.

There is factual evidence of the drowning of a resident, the hotelier Charles Budina's sister-in-law, in the now-drained swimming pool, when Kilmacurragh House functioned as the Park Hotel in the 1940s. This grim litany of premature deaths, death by accident and political reprisal culminates in the fatal injuries sustained by Major Charles Annesley Acton and Captain Reginald Thomas Annesley Ball-Acton, two heroic heirs to Kilmacurragh, on active service with the British army during World War I. Some of the gardeners and labourers also died on active service. This history lends a particular poignancy to the garden, especially in May and June, when the Broad Walk is strewn with the crimson petals of *Rhododendron 'altaclerense'* planted by Janet Acton. These 'petals of remembrance' are local reminders of the poppies of Flanders. In the walled garden, once a nursery

for new plants, there are three rather cramped mature ginkgo trees which were never transplanted and which remain a grim testimony to the tragic toll taken by war.

A memorial garden

The late Charles Acton (1914–99), the last heir to have lived in Kilmacurragh, paid tribute to a forester named Eric Joyce, killed in a tragic accident in 1983, who had participated in the restoration of the garden after years of decline. A commemorative plaque has been erected in his memory behind the mansion.

Knowledge of these historical facts associated with the garden prompts reflection on the many hands who have moulded it and makes it a memorial not only to those who are buried in it but also to all those who once lived and worked there.

3

THE RELUCTANT CROMWELLIAN

'The felons of the Leinster Mountains'

In the 1515 Report on the State of Ireland, the area that was to become County Wicklow in the early seventeenth century is described as not being 'subject to the king's laws', a reference to the cycle of raids and counter-raids by 'the felons of the Leinster Mountains, the O'Byrnes and the O'Tooles'. This situation called for a change in governmental strategy. Settlements of mainly Protestant English people were deemed a likely solution, resulting in what was one of the earliest English settlements in eastern Wicklow—namely that which took place in the reign of Edward VI (1547–53).[25] The new settlers found County Wicklow a place where 'war was endemic', mainly because of its vast mountainous hinterland, which provided secure refuge for the dispossessed Irish. The defeat of the native Irish clans towards the end of Elizabeth's reign (*c.* 1603) was followed by an intensification of settlement in the following centuries. In Wicklow, L.M. Cullen recounts, 'Protestant settlement was extensive on and under the eastern shoulder of the mountain ranges from Delgany and Enniskerry to Templetown (Roundwood) inland, and to Dunganstown near the coast … A third of the population of the county was Protestant with large settlements in Rathdrum, Arklow and around Tinahely and Carnew.'[26] This saturation policy gave some stability to the settlers, who, according to Rolf Loeber,[27] knew how to exploit the wood resources of Ireland, and those of Shillelagh, Co. Wicklow, in particular.[28] Eileen McCracken corroborates this view, stating that 'one of the inducements used to persuade settlers to come to Ireland at the end of the 16th century was the profits offered by the exploitation of the woods'.[29] We cannot exclude this inducement as having had an appeal for the Acton family in the following century.

Exploitation of wood resources—the insurrection of 1641

Since the mid-1500s an intensive timber industry had developed in County Wicklow, which in turn led to several auxiliary industries there, typically the leather-tanning industry and the iron industry, which utilised spoiled wood to produce charcoal

PREVIOUS PAGE A broken oak bole on the 'Oak Avenue'.

BOTTOM LEFT Detail of bark of a Lawson's cypress (*Chamaecyparis lawsoniana*).

BOTTOM RIGHT The rippled bark of a leaning yew (*Taxus baccata*).

LEFT Two of the thousands of Scots pines (*Pinus sylvestris*) planted by William Acton (1789–1854). This tree species was introduced into Ireland by the Cromwellians.

the English navy. Wood was needed for pipe staves and barrel staves for both the home and the European market, and for the building of galleys in Scotland; sawmills were established under licence. A lot of money was made at the cost of serious deforestation where replanting was neglected. The attempted coup of 1641, however, and the protracted hostilities for the following eight years during the civil war in England resulted in heavy losses for the industrialists. Loeber tells of a mariner, Richard Dickson, who reported that, 'as a result of the rebellion, he had lost 2,500 feet of 12-inch planks intended for shipbuilding'.[30]

The difficulties that had arisen in England between King Charles I and the intolerant Protestant parliament prompted the 'Old English'—Catholics in Ireland—and the Catholic Irish in Ulster to take advantage of the situation to further their cause. Their objectives were the full recognition of Catholicism and the restoration of confiscated lands to the Irish, in the name of which they mounted an insurrection in 1641, which had spread from Ulster to the entire island by 1642. Years of fighting came to an end with the trial and execution of Charles I in 1649, and the English parliament then turned its attention to Ireland. There had been wildly exaggerated reports of the 'bloody massacre' of Ulster settlers in 1641. The most recent research indicates that several thousand Protestant settlers had been killed. When Oliver Cromwell came to Ireland with his Puritan army in 1649 he was bent on avenging that massacre and other perceived rebel atrocities.

to fire the forges. The cost of timber production was cheaper than in England. The added amenities of the ports of Wicklow, Arklow and Wexford in the adjoining county, from which timber products could be exported, made this industry economically attractive. Certain woods were reserved for the crown, such as the oak trees in Shillelagh, Co. Wicklow, or were marked out for

A family dynasty established on confiscated lands: Cromwellian confiscation and redistribution of lands

The reprisals for the 1641 rebellion were particularly brutal and would lead to further confiscation of lands belonging to the rebels and their sympathisers by Oliver Cromwell. According to the Settlement of Ireland Act 1652, penalties including death and land confiscation were imposed on participants and bystanders, i.e. those who had aided and abetted the rebels of 1641 in any way. These confiscations are illustrated in the map opposite. The ensuing 'plantation', like all previous ones, was based on the English conviction that 'land was the source of wealth and the basis of power'.[31]

In the 1640s the Acton family rented land which was subsequently confiscated and awarded to Cromwellian lieutenants. According to the Hearth Roll of 1669, Thomas Acton (d. 1716), father of the founder of the family dynasty in Kilmacurragh (also called Thomas and referred to as Thomas II), is registered as having paid hearth tax for Bog Hall and Kilcandra two years before his son Thomas's birth (1671). In that same year a Thomas Leigh paid hearth tax for Kilmacurragh. Documentation indicates that the Actons leased the land from the Byrne family some time *before* the Cromwellian redistribution of those lands (indicated in the Down Survey map of 1655), made as a reprisal for Byrne's perceived rebel involvement in the insurrection. The lands in question were granted to Hugh Montgomery and Sir Richard Parsons of Birr Castle, who became Viscount Rosse[32] and to whom Thomas Acton subsequently paid rent.[33] These gentlemen, one infers, were thus rewarded for services rendered to Cromwell, whose lieutenants they were (and possible creditors also). On being dispossessed of their lands, however, the (O')Byrnes did not move far away but merely to their estate in Cronybyrne, Rathdrum, according to Richard Pine. The Cronybyrne estate included several woods in the Vale of Clara. In the old Catholic graveyard at Castletimon, Dunganstown, it is noticeable that

BELOW LEFT 'Where the leaf falls let it rest' (Keats).

BELOW RIGHT Patterned rhododendron bark.

many by the name of Byrne were buried there in the 1700s and 1800s, which arguably points to the continuous presence of the extended family in the general area.

Charles, the reluctant Cromwellian

From his twentieth-century perspective, Charles Acton (1914–99), the last heir of Kilmacurragh and well-known music critic, was dismayed by the apparent Cromwellian connection of his family. Any connection with the indiscriminate inhumanity with which the Irish royalist supporters were treated by Cromwell and his Puritan army, and which was indelibly imprinted on the folk memory of the Irish, was distasteful to him. He always asserted that the Actons had been

in County Wicklow since the 1640s and thus possibly even prior to the Cromwellian campaign (1649–50). It is fascinating to speculate on his ancestors' motivation for leaving their Shropshire village and coming to Ireland, and to Wicklow in particular. It is unlikely that the Actons, who would leave their house in Peter Street, Dublin, to visit their property in Wicklow,[34] were attracted to that county exclusively by leisure activities such as deer- and game-hunting. It is more likely that they were part of the seventeenth-century intensive settlement of Wicklow, which Ken Hannigan tells us 'was followed by two centuries in which the mineral and timber resources of the county drew large numbers of entrepreneurs and artisans'.[35]

When the Acton family visited County Wicklow for what one assumes were sporting activities, they 'occupied a small shooting box near

the Deputy's Pass …'. Afterwards they had a small residence, 'Bog Hall', the ruins of which still existed in the 1800s near Kilcandra[36] on land which they leased from Sir Richard Parsons (Lord Rosse). 'There also they had a cock-pit'—cock-fighting was a rather bloody eighteenth-century sport traditionally described as 'organised for gentlemen by gentlemen'. An intriguing entry in the Kilmacurragh Book also informs us that they kept a Fool for their amusement, like their neighbours the Tighes. (The practice of maintaining a full-time jester died out among the English aristocracy around the 1800s.) Janet Acton (1824–1906), the family archivist, indicated that the actual location of the house at Kilcandra was behind the forge, where the remains of the cock-pit could still be seen. Bog Hall was then three days' journey from Dublin, the resting places being Kilcoole and Bray. There are other references in the Kilmacurragh Book to the Peter Street property in Dublin, which was retained after the permanent move to County Wicklow and was a refuge for the family during the 1798 rebellion.

While initially it would appear that the main interest of Thomas II, the founder of the Kilmacurragh dynasty, was in farming, land acquisition and amenity planting, his son William's purchase of woods in Clara, just north of

Rathdrum, in 1758 points to the family's recognition of the wealth potential of the timber industry. William advertised 'its timber … for sale in Saunder's Newsletter', and Richard Pine further writes that Clara 'would provide a commercial interest in timber [for the family] that continued up to the 1930s'.[37]

Incontrovertibly Cromwellian

Charles's Aunt Irene, as Charles observed, 'is determined that we are Cromwellian; I suppose if we are we are, but one doesn't like the idea much!'[38] Nevertheless, his family, while being 'of Ireland', to use Charles's expression, served the British Empire; as professional soldiers they enlisted in her wars, and therefore could conceivably have been in Cromwell's army.[39]

Charles's insistence that his family's arrival in Ireland was pre-Cromwellian[40] (1649–50) does not preclude an eventual strong Cromwellian connection. In fact, the first clue comes from Edward Acton (d. 1656), son of the first recorded Thomas Acton in Ireland and Thomas II's uncle.[41] Richard Pine infers from Edward's will, probated in 1656, that he had been a Cromwellian soldier, given that he bequeathed his arrears of pay to his father. Cromwellian soldiers were often 'paid' in land seized from the native Irish. Other incontrovertible evidence of Cromwellian

connections is that Thomas Acton II (Edward's nephew), the founder of the Acton dynasty in Kilmacurragh, married Elinor Kempston, the daughter of a Cromwellian soldier, Colonel Nicholas Kempston. A generation later, *his* son William would marry Jane Parsons of Birr Castle, a detail which points to a close connection between the two families. There is every likelihood that the Actons and the Parsons came to Ireland within about twenty years of each other. Birr Castle, seat of the Parsons family, was granted to Sir Laurence Parsons in 1620. The two families were English, socially compatible and Protestant. Richard Parsons was granted confiscated land in Wicklow by Cromwell for services rendered during his campaign after the 1641 rebellion. Forty-five years later, in 1697, this land was first leased to Thomas Acton II (1671–1750), though there is evidence that the Actons were renting Kilmacurragh from the (O')Byrnes prior to the redistribution of *their* lands to Richard Parsons. The Clanchy map of 1708 indicates what may have been an artist's impression of the mansion on the site before its completion in 1716. There is every likelihood that Thomas II lived in a more modest house on the lands of Kilmacurragh before building his mansion there. His father continued to live in the old home in the adjoining Kilcandra.

Thus the lands of Kilmacurragh were formally leased to Thomas Acton II more than 40 years after the Cromwellian campaign and 37 years after the restoration of the monarchy (1660). If some loose arrangement existed prior to that, such property transfers to local landowners were common and protected by the Adventurers Act,[42] which confirmed transfer of ownership. Decisions made regarding land during Cromwell's Protectorate were not generally reversed after the restoration of the monarchy. Logically, then, given Charles's conviction that the Acton elders had been in Ireland since the early 1640s, they may have witnessed the insurrection of 1641 and the

subsequent upheavals generated by the Cromwellian campaign in Ireland, and may even have participated in it as Cromwellian soldiers. Certainly, being English and Protestant, they were the eventual beneficiaries of the ensuing land redistribution.

Charles's dismay at the Cromwellian link is an indicator of how much he, though belonging to a family of English gentlemen of Irish birth, mainly educated in England, had grown into a sense of Irishness, 'of being of Ireland'. It had taken several generations of Actons to identify with Ireland in the way that Charles did; he saw it as his country and felt that his place was in Ireland, within Irish society. Indeed, he went on to make valuable contributions to the music culture of the country, but his comments regarding the 'county' patrons of the Kilmacurragh Park Hotel (1932–44) were rather sceptical, if not patronising, in his recognition of cultural difference, as he queried whether 'the polarity of "us" and "the rest" could ever be resolved'.[43] Nevertheless, Charles's longstanding friend, Richard Pine, in his Appreciation[44] of the music critic after his death, described him as 'epitomising the *rapprochement* of classes, creeds and commitments', something which was amply borne out by his artistic efforts to create a new Ireland.

ABOVE A beech near the Broad Walk in the May sunshine.

4

THE SEVENTEENTH–EIGHTEENTH CENTURY

ABOVE Maytime on the entrance driveway.

Thomas Acton II (1671–1750) and his wife, Elinor Kempston

Thomas Acton II (1671–1750), high sheriff for County Wicklow, is the third recorded Thomas Acton in the family entry in Burke's *Landed gentry of Ireland* 'and presumed the third generation of Actons living in Ireland'.[45]

In 1697, at the age of 26, Thomas began building the Queen Anne[46] or 'Early Georgian' mansion[47] in Kilmacurragh, which his father had leased in 1677 from Sir Richard Parsons. The land comprised 81 acres and was close to the house in which he had been reared in Kilcandra. He knew his family history and that of the lands in which he had grown up. He would have been aware of the distinctive socio-religious character of the area owing to the saturation plantation policy of the English crown up to 1600 and later to the Cromwellian redistribution of lands after the rising of 1641. It is likely that Thomas already had a dwelling of his own on the lands before constructing the more imposing mansion on the present site. The Knight of Glin[48] writes how after the Protestant victory at the Battle of the Boyne in 1690 a 'British colonial Ascendancy' government in Ireland engendered a sense of confidence in the 'country houses and demesnes', whose owners would by implication have been encouraged to invest a lot in their homes. This would explain why Thomas felt secure in building one of the first unfortified houses to be constructed in Ireland by a member of the Ascendancy class.

The conclusive 'setting' of the lands was formalised on completion of the construction of the mansion. In January 1715 the Honourable Richard Lord Viscount Rosse, 'pursuant to an act of parlim't', was enabled to 'sett' the lands of Kilmacurragh, Knocknottin and Ballybeg to Thomas Acton. On completion of the mansion, Thomas obtained from Richard, Viscount Rosse, by deeds dated 13 February and 10 May 1716, leases for lives renewable for ever of lands in County Wicklow.

The text on the 1715 map (opposite) illustrating the nucleus of Thomas Acton's estate reads:

> 'A mapp of Killmacurragh, Knocknottin & Ballybegg in the parish of Dunganstown Barrony of Arklow & County of Wicklow now sett to Thomas Acton Esq. by the Court appointed by the Rt. Honourable Richd. Lord Viscount Rosse pursuant to an act of parlim't in England to Enable him to dispose and sett of the sd. Estate and surveyed by their order in the month of January 1715. (Signed) Peter Duff'.[49]

Details of the payment arrangements make curious reading: there was a payment of £87, plus an annual rent of £30 to be paid, as Peter Pearson recounts, 'at Strongbow's tombe in Christ Church

LEFT March daffodils and naturalised crocuses on the front lawn.

ABOVE Autumn leaves lap the angled horizontals.

ABOVE RIGHT Angled splash into the lily pond.

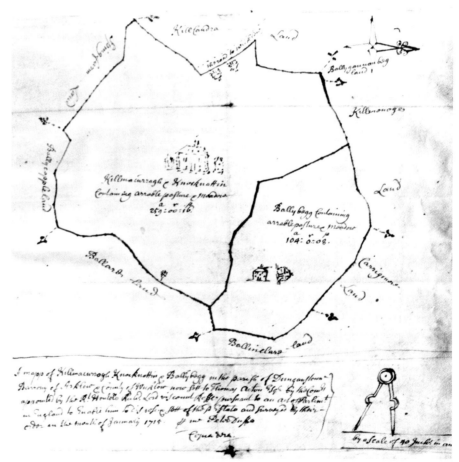

RIGHT 1715 map of estate. This image is reproduced courtesy of the National Library of Ireland [Ref. 21 F71].

Dublin', in 'two even moities at the Feast of St Michael the Archangel and at the feast of the Assumption of the Blessed Virgin'. This was apparently a time-honoured convention among certain classes for sealing an agreement.[50]

To complement his mansion, Thomas laid out a wide, gravelled sweep in front of the house. In time he also built a double coach-house, two stables, a barn, a cowhouse and other outbuildings, as well as allocating 40 acres for a Deer Park with its surrounding ditch or ha-ha, featuring its inner side below ground level to avoid interrupting the view. The Deer Park appears already well established in Neville's map of 1760. Apparently several Englishmen in the 1630s, recounts Loeber,[51] 'sought out County Wicklow for the creation of deerparks'. Documentary evidence concerning the 'rebuilding' of the coach-house in 1729 implies that out-offices were contemporaneous with the mansion.

ABOVE An easterly view looking towards Castletimon and the locally named 'Sleananus' (the Gaelic name meaning 'the hill of the screen' or 'the belt of the trees') to the right. In the foreground is the front lawn, once the site of the monks' graveyard, where wild flowers now proliferate in summer.

Kilmacurragh mansion—its architectural design

As already mentioned, on the lands of Kilmacurragh there was evidence of a pre-Christian settlement in the form of a rath and the ruins of a monastic settlement. Thomas built his mansion almost exactly on the site of the ruined monastic church of St Mochorog. It was a typical middle-sized house of the early eighteenth century, compatible with minor gentry status. The two-storey, five-bay house with breakfront centre comprised five reception rooms and eight bedrooms. It is believed to have been built after a design by the famous English architect Sir William Robinson, whose signature detail, the triangular-headed attic window, is still clearly visible in the large pediment.[52] Although records indicate that building began in 1697, both the last heir, Charles Acton (1914–99), and the architect Maurice Craig

classify the residence as early eighteenth-century or 'Early Georgian', a term used to describe the tail-end of the Queen Anne style. This style, which gradually became more severe in its lines and architectural detail, is still evident even in the remnants of the mansion today, especially in the high-pitched roof on a wooden bracket cornice, the good quoins (external angles of its outer walls) and the windows away from the corners. Craig comments that 'the core of the original house (extended in the nineteenth century) seemed to be the product of a single designer working out a single architectural conception at a particular time'.[53]

The east-facing mansion commanded the route from Wicklow inland to Rathdrum (referred to as the Coach Road), for which 100 years later, in 1818, Lt Col. William Acton MP (1789–1854) had a judicial permission (presentment) to close off. Later, in 1848, as part of famine relief works,

RIGHT Kilmacurragh House c. 1932.
Included (l. to r.) are James Taylor, Isabel Digues La Touche (mother of the last heir, Charles Acton), Mr Peake and Hugh Digues La Touche, Charles's stepfather. Both wings were later additions. Note the timber door-case and the wooden cornice.
Photograph: Charles Acton. Courtesy of the Library, NBG, Glasnevin, and the OPW.

ABOVE The timber door-case.
The house was already partially derelict.
Photograph: David Davison, 1983. Courtesy of
the photographer.
The elaborately moulded door-case with pilasters
featuring, as Bence-Jones described, 'a repetition
of reentrants (inward-pointing angles), the
entablature (the horizontal, moulded projection
crowning the door) curving upwards in an
exuberant Baroque way'.[57]

ABOVE RIGHT Entrance hall and stairs, 1983.
Photograph courtesy of the photographer, David
Davison. This photograph was taken in the 1980s,
when the mansion was already in decline, but it
gives a good idea of the original interior, although
the tiled floor was a later addition, according to
Dr David Griffin of the Irish Architectural Archive.
The once-elegant staircase was made of pitch-
pine, with distinctive barley-sugar balusters. An
impressive specimen of a giant elk's antlers, 9ft in
length, hung on the staircase leading from the
entrance hall.

over 100 years after its construction, it was he too
who added '2 single-storey, 2 bay projecting and
overlapping wings' in the same style as the centre,
'so that they might pass as contemporary with it,
or at any rate, as early c18th additions'.[54]

'The estate was called West Aston from the
middle of the 18th century to the middle of the
19th century.' [55]

'My new mansion house'

Thomas carefully costed the ongoing expenditure
on his new mansion, together with general
improvements on the land:

> '1707–1709 Estimate of expenditure on
> building ditches and other improvements
> made to the lands. Total £2,020 of which the
> principal item "My new mansion house"
> accounts for £1,500'[56] (c. £200,000 in 2013,
> according to the retail price index).

ABOVE Detailed entry in Thomas's account book. This image is reproduced courtesy of the National Library of Ireland.
This itemises, among other things, the cost of materials and services agreed on for his house: 'masonry work for the double chimney ... brickwork computed to 43...', payment for the service of 'drawing sand' 'for a mantletree', 'for 900 of bricks . . .', 'hogsheads of lime' and '50 foot of glasing [*sic*] windows'.

RIGHT Chinese evergreen magnolia blossom (*Magnolia delavayi*).
This tree, which grows at the back of the mansion, was planted by Sir Frederick and Phyllis, Lady Moore, from the then Royal Botanic Gardens, Glasnevin, Dublin, in March 1919. It was propagated from an E.H. Wilson original at Glasnevin.

Actual details from Thomas's 1717 accounts ledger regarding certain materials and services connected to the 'new mansion' project us into the scene, the dashing, slanting style of his handwriting and the minutiae of the details creating a sense of immediacy.

The house 'took years to complete', as Janet Acton recorded in the family archive almost 150 years later—a lengthy enterprise that had evidently entered the family folklore. In fact, it took twenty years to complete. 'Not such a remarkable thing,' writes Charles D. Lyons, 'as it regularly took 20 years to complete such buildings; it is reasonable to assume that the house itself was only completed around 1716, the date for which the title deeds are compiled.'[58]

300 years after construction

Such is the sad condition of Thomas's meticulously constructed mansion today that it seems appropriate to digress at this point, to speak for the house that cannot speak for itself.

More than 300 years after its construction, one's embarrassment at its neglect is somewhat mitigated by the fact that at least we know what the mansion once looked like. We are fortunate that such an early mansion, 'one of only two Queen Anne Houses left in the country', as Charles Lyons points out, has attracted the attention of twentieth- and 21st-century architects, photographers, postgraduate students of architecture and writers interested in heritage buildings, especially in that period when it was clearly under threat. While their attention did not save the building, we are indebted to their professional observations and photographs of the building for enabling us, at least in imagination, to put substance back into what is now a ghostly remnant.

Signs of decay were already too plainly evident by the time David Davison, photographer, Mark

Bence-Jones, recognised chronicler of the disappearing world of the Ascendancy, Maurice Craig, architect, and postgraduate architecture student Charles Declan Lyons recorded their comments.

A stout construction

Twentieth-century commentators on the mansion—when it was already in a ruinous condition—noted the quality of the materials used and the massiveness of the construction. Its sheer survival in the Irish climate testifies to its sturdiness. Craig comments on the shortage of timber owing to the destruction of forests in the seventeenth century, which became even more acute in the eighteenth century, 'except in or near sea ports, where good Baltic timber was available'. A Kilmacurragh account dated 1730 refers to the purchase of foreign timber for construction purposes, so there is every likelihood that the timber used in the earlier construction of the house was imported, perhaps from the Baltic.

Opposite page

Top left Japanese red cedar (*Cryptomeria japonica*), one of the fine redwoods on the Glade. This is not a true cedar but is one of the redwood family, introduced, despite its name, from China in 1842.

Top right Chinese fir (*Cunninghamia lanceolata*).

Bottom Giant elk's antlers at NBG, Glasnevin. This impressive specimen of a giant elk's antlers, 9ft in length, hung on the staircase leading from the entrance hall. It had been found in a bog in Kiltymon and now hangs in the reception area at the National Botanic Gardens, Glasnevin.

A significant use of timber

Maurice Craig thought that the use of timber in the construction of the Kilmacurragh mansion was significant. He inferred, on inspection, that seventeenth-century buildings must have been of stouter construction than those built in later centuries, because only those of that description would have survived. He found that, while Kilmacurragh was 'falling down' in 1976, the roof structure was 'massive and apparently original ... with principals at appropriate intervals, and purlins (beams) of a size which would be expected in a similar English house'.[59] There were oak sash-windows too, many of which still survive. Craig observes that the 'cornice and doorcase are of timber—this must have once been common practice—few survived into the 20th century in our climate'. The wooden door-case—long since fallen off and decayed—because of its highly decorative style was one of the outstanding features of the mansion which Davison's photograph recorded just in time. This elaborate feature, according to Craig, gave the lie to the notion that there was a lack of variation in country house door-cases of that time. He cites both

TOP The skeletal remains of a once classically elegant mansion.
The two wings were later additions by Lt Col. William Acton MP (1789–1854) as part of famine relief works in 1848.

ABOVE Detail of the north wall of the mansion, featuring stones possibly salvaged from the ruined church on the site and red bricks of local manufacture.

Kilmacurragh and Eyre Court as illustrating the fact that quite the opposite was true.

The Knight of Glin[60] comments that the 1700s were notable for the baroque influence of some French carvers, the three Tabary brothers, who were part of the Huguenot community in Dublin at that time and whose work in the Royal Hospital, Kilmainham, set the highest standard in their field. It is quite conceivable that both the elaborate carved door-case and the staircase at Kilmacurragh were carved in Dublin by members of that school.

Charles D. Lyons carried out a comprehensive postgraduate 'working study'[61] on the mansion in 1990, almost a decade after the Davison photographs were taken. He noted the following features of the mansion: 'a spacious hall with its black and white quarry tile floor laid to pattern, an elegant staircase made entirely of pitch pine' with distinctive barley-sugar balusters[62] (pitch-pine would have been used in preference to oak, as it was easier to carve). He also noted the black marble

fireplaces with the traditional seventeenth-century corner position, good examples of which were in the drawing-room and in the large partitioned room off the entrance hall. This placing of the fireplaces economised on the number of chimneys required, as well as facilitating the circulation of the heat from the fire and giving the rooms an interesting shape.[63] Lyons comments that 'the floors were of pitch pine and the unplastered walls were field-panelled in wood against the damp. The kitchen and the butler's pantry were in the basement, with servants' quarters located in the attics in the north west corner of the mansion. Access to the kitchen in the basement was via a

BELOW Hartweg's pine (*Pinus hartwegii*), introduced in 1839 by Carl Theodore Hartweg.

separate service stairs. Outside the kitchen were the kitchen and donkey yards.'

'The window cills were of granite while the windows themselves were of oak throughout … the front door case is of timber, the façade is of rubble stone construction,' he noted.[64] The roof slates were of excellent quality. The official view of the government after inspection of the property (1990) was that 'the roof slates and the fire places were of real commercial value', but that the building was 'uneconomical to repair and apart from the east façade has no architectural features which would justify preservation'.[65]

Rebuilding of the coach-house and stables in 1729

> 'An agreement between Thos. Acton and Thomas Burke stonedigger/stone drawer to draw stone for building a paddock wall [surrounding the present visitors' car park] at least 7ft high on the lands of Kilmacurra.'[66]

Also attributed to Thomas Acton is the building of the Walled Garden with inbuilt heating system and orangery, though they do not feature in Neville's map of 1760. Thus Thomas's building programme was substantially complete, enhancing his status as a gentleman landowner.

A geographical perspective

The Neville map (opposite, below) places the Acton demesne, then known as 'Westaston Demesne', in topographical perspective, showing the mansion and surrounding pleasure garden, the fenced Deer Park and the eastern boundary of the old Coach Road (marked in green), later closed by Col. William Acton in 1818. At an acute angle to it lies the road to Kilcandra, where Thomas grew up

ABOVE Segment of the wall of the Walled Garden, showing the structure of the wood-fired heating system used in the once-adjoining orangery.

OPPOSITE PAGE, TOP The curve of the Walled Garden.

OPPOSITE PAGE, BELOW The well-worn eighteenth-century threshold from the paddock (present car park) into the old coach-house yard.

and where his father continued to live, as did many of the estate workers. Westaston Hill lies to the south. 'Bog Hall' in Ballygannonbeg (B:ganonbeg on map), a townland adjoining Kilmacurragh, was where the original family home was situated.

Marriage to Elinor

Thomas married Elinor Kempston, daughter of Colonel Nicholas Kempston, with whom he would have four children: Grace, William (1711–79), Elinor and Alice.

BELOW Neville's map, 1760.
The 1760 Jacob Neville map of 'Westaston Demesne', by which name Kilmacurragh was known during part of the 1700s until the mid-1800s, when Thomas Acton IV reverted to the name 'Kilmacurragh'. Note the well-defined, enclosed deer park. The Coach Road is marked in green. The linear stippled features are explained in the key or legend of the map as 'corn'. 'There was a lot of arable cultivation in Co. Wicklow at the time, however, so such indications may be more a form of decoration than a precise survey of arable and pasture lands.' [67]
Courtesy of the Map Library, Trinity College, Dublin.

'Clothing' the interior of the mansion

ABOVE *Colchicum autumnale* 'album', with sedum 'Autumn joy'.

The interior of Thomas and Elinor's mansion was no doubt typical of medium-sized country houses of the time. Given the classical, spare beauty of the design of the mansion and the quality of the building materials used, the furnishings must have been proportionately elegant and typical of seventeenth-century Irish furniture.

The entrance hall would have had a wooden floor (the black and white tiles in Davison's photographs were a later addition, according to Dr David Griffin[68]), a Kilkenny marble fireplace in a corner position, panelled walls hung with the ubiquitous elk antlers, family portraits, pier-glasses and candle sconces mounted on the walls, and a central hall lantern hanging from the ornate plaster ceiling. As well as in the entrance hall, it would have been common to use such lanterns in passages and on staircases because they shielded candles from draughts and people from unwelcome drips of grease.[69] Presiding over the entrance hall on the staircase was an impressive specimen of a giant elk's antlers, 9ft in length. An early twentieth-century novel entitled *Eve's doctor*, inspired by the author Signe Toksvig's[70] visits to the mansion in the 1900s, when Lady Phillimore was the lessee, describes the fictional entrance hall hung with '… Zulu cowhide shields and a full cemetery of horned animal heads'. This last description fits neatly with the family's passion for deer-hunting.

Typically, the dining-room would have included a large oak or mahogany table, high-backed chairs in walnut or mahogany, a sideboard and serving tables. The Kilmacurragh Book relates

that Jane Parsons, who married Thomas's son William Acton (1711–79), brought carved high-backed chairs from Birr Castle, as well as a precious cabinet gifted to her by Queen Caroline (1683–1737), for whom she was a lady-in-waiting. Such cabinets were used to display fine china and glass, silver plate and family memorabilia such as medals. There is also a reference to Jane's 'dressing tray and dressing case', which were fine enough to merit special mention.

Auction inventories for similar mansions of the time included cane-seated chairs, drop-leaf tables, desks and fitted bookcases, settees, matching chairs, upholstered stools in rich colours and pier-glasses. The bedrooms would typically have had four-poster beds of oak or mahogany with hangings that matched the curtains, tallboys, looking-glasses with gilt frames, bedside and night tables, and a pot commode. Large chests were used for linens and candles. The Kilmacurragh Book further helps us with a few token references to 'clothe' the interior of the mansion with furniture,

TOP Lady's mantle *Alchemilla* and geranium 'Jolly Bee'.

ABOVE Geranium 'Jolly Bee'.

hangings and recorded gifts accumulated down the generations: there were wedding presents of fine Waterford glass gifted to Thomas Acton III and Sidney Davis in the late 1700s, a circular inlaid table that belonged to Martha, Thomas's sister; fine china; and a collection of ancestral family portraits in oils, among which was a portrait of Thomas Maule, surveyor of customs in Kilkenny in 1629. (The Acton family can be traced back to the twelfth century, according to the late Charles Acton.) There was a library of books, one of which, Sir Joseph Hooker's *Rhododendrons of Sikkim Himalaya*,[71] was kept inside the door by Thomas Acton IV in the late 1800s to verify rhododendron species. There was a nursery with children's toys, including the late Charles Acton's rocking-horse and music box. Such meagre details are but tiny clues to the intimate family life lived in a once-elegant middle-sized family mansion.[72] The catalogue of the auctioneers Mealy's of Castlecomer, Co. Kilkenny, of the sale of the late Charles Acton's home on 26–27 June 2001 included an eighteenth-century pocket globe, 3in. in diameter, part of a collection of globes made in 1750 by William King of Dublin. Enclosed in a fish-skin case lined with celestial charts, it was valued at £4,000–£6,000 and would have been a sample of the precious family heirlooms that were exhibited in display cabinets in the mansion.

It is interesting to learn that Charles Acton never 'particularly liked the house'. He found it cold and 'impossible to heat'. His knowledgeable comment that 'its interest is in its age' is widely endorsed.

The Dutch gardeners

Thomas's decision to build his mansion on the site (allegedly on the very foundations) of the ruined monastery church, with an east-facing orientation and partial view of the Wicklow coast, and with

ABOVE Sedum 'Autumn Joy'.

OPPOSITE PAGE The Glade, very possibly originally laid out by Dutch gardeners in the eighteenth century.
Now flanked by some of the finest heritage trees in the garden, including giant redwoods and podocarps, it reaches down to the pond and guides the eye to the view beyond.

Westaston Hill to the south-west, influenced the development of the surrounding pleasure gardens. The gently undulating topographical features determined the broad lines of the garden design, something which he entrusted to Dutch gardeners,[73] following the fashion of the day. After the accession of William III, the picturesque Dutch garden art enjoyed great popularity for a time, before being generally derided. Thus Thomas, like other landowners anxious to emulate the royals, introduced typical Dutch features such as an encircling canal linking smaller hedged subdivisions of the garden, pleached (interlacing) hedging, grand avenues and glades with views beyond the garden. It was essentially a schematic, angular style, the very opposite of the wilder, more natural, Robinsonian style[74] of garden that eventually evolved in Kilmacurragh in the second half of the nineteenth century, during which the moulding of the arboretum, as distinct from

widespread tree-planting, took shape and both pleasure gardens and arboretum reached their peak.

The emphasis was on symmetry and regularity—a 'stiff garden', as Robinson might see it. The Dutch-style pleasure gardens extended to the fenced Deer Park, a common demesne feature since the 1600s; there was one in the nearby Kilruddery demesne, outside Bray. The busy old Coach Road, an important conduit from the hinterland to Wicklow port, marked the eastern boundary of the estate.

The undulating upland site of Kilmacurragh would not have been ideal, in any case, for a garden style best suited to flat land and, understandably, only a few hints of that 'golden age' of Dutch garden design have survived. These include a grand avenue, the old unused carriageway, recently (2014) replanted with Chile-sourced monkey-puzzle trees, which may have been laid on an older Dutch foundation, the wide sweep in front of the house and the Glade, extending from the south window of the mansion to the pond, with the mandatory view beyond into the Deer Park. At that time there were two monks' fish-ponds. Occasional quasi-enclosed mini-'compartments' in today's garden are faint echoes, too, of that seventeenth–eighteenth-century Dutch style. The 40/50-acre Deer Park—now a Coillte research centre for commercial trees—was traditionally stocked with deer for hunting purposes, a practice which persisted into the late 1800s and was a great attraction for house guests. There is a beguiling description of the deer left by one of the visiting admirers, Frederick William Burbidge, writing in the 1800s:

> '...here and there through the tree trunks you get delightful glimpses of the fallow deer in the sunny park below, some displaying themselves on the short grass, while others more timid of the wandering stranger take shelter in the thickets of gorse . . . or canter away through

the groves of tall grey barked Alders that are such a notable feature here'.[75]

Thomas's mansion, with its coach-house and stables, walled garden, pleasure gardens, inherited monks' fish-ponds and Deer Park, reflected his organisational ability, wealth and ambition for the future. In the course of time, good husbandry, advantageous marriage alliances and land acquisition did indeed earn the family the status of landed gentry, a fact affirmed by Charles Acton's entry in the 1958 edition of Burke's *Landed gentry of Ireland*.

Thomas active in local affairs

Thomas was active in local affairs and was one of the three grand jurors responsible for a new workhouse in Rathdrum in the borough of Wicklow, which opened in 1715. It was 'designed to create work for the poor' and was specifically aimed at 'the encouragement of the Hempen and Flaxen manufacture', something later promoted by the Dublin Society.[76] Thomas himself grew flax, as the field known as 'the bleaching field' testifies.

Passionate about trees—a father's advice

There had been great demand historically for Irish wood. Apart from local wood-dependent industries, as Eileen McCracken explains, the Great Fire of London in 1666 created a demand for Irish oak, and the English navy also required a lot of timber.[77]

While Thomas Acton's father—also named Thomas (d. 1716)—continued to reside in the original family home in nearby Kilcandra, he gave fatherly advice to his son, recorded in an early extant notebook. He reminded him:

> 'to prepare for grafting walnut and chestnut, oak

ABOVE Centre: another fine specimen of Mexican
cypress (*Cupressus lusitanica*).

and ash and also to get w[hite] oates ych [which] can [be] threshed & made money of'.[78]

These were the words of a practical man who understood the craft of tree maintenance as well as the commercial value of trees and specific crops. They also allude to Thomas's existing tree stock. With such an ancestor it is little wonder that trees and their cultivation were in the very blood of successive generations of Actons. In fact, Thomas became one of the first landowners in Ireland to plant trees in any great number, thereby enriching his demesne and enhancing the local environment. Sadly, his father, his guide and mentor, died six months after the completion of the mansion. This fact, together with the burial in Rathdrum and the funeral expenses incurred, is recorded matter-of-factly in Thomas's accounts ledger.

Thomas's father died on 10 November 1716. His death and burial expenses were recorded as follows:

'My father dyed at Kilcandra on Saturday the 10th Nov., 1716, and was buryed in Rathdrum Church on Monday the 13th of Nov., 1716'.

Items costed included:

'10 crape hatbands and ribbon to tie them up, black cloath to cover the coffin
And clasps and hinges, a dozen of shamy gloves, a cask of white wine . . . 19 pairs of sheepskin gloves for men and women . . . black and white silk stuff for a gowne . . . muslin hankerchefes . . .'

RIGHT Oak in autumn, the driveway.

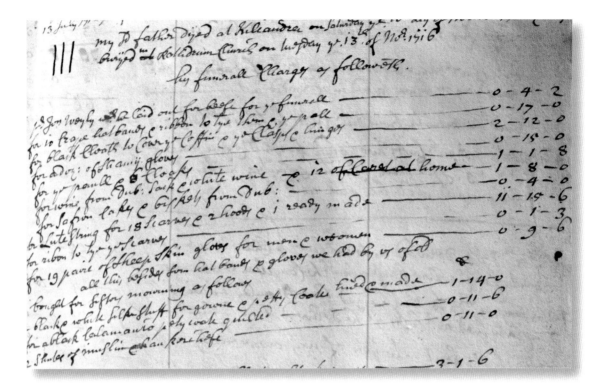

These meticulously detailed entries give an insight into Thomas's social status and quantity of servants, as well as highlighting his punctiliousness and matter-of-fact nature.

Entries in an early extant notebook, observes Richard Pine, show that Thomas was a hands-on farmer who bought and sold sheep and hired farm-hands. Items confirming this down-to-earth method of conducting his business appear in his 1716 accounts, a photographed page from which is printed overleaf. Everything is recorded, in a hand that sometimes defies decipherment, from selling cocks of hay and bandy filleys (*sic*) to paying his bills for ale and bread:

> 'Jan: 1716 Sold to Danny Doyle the 3 yrold black filley for 30 s pd.'
> 'March 1716 Sold Jon Wyley yrold cock of hay at Kil(candra?) for 25 s which he paid me'
> 'Sold the old grey mare to Robert Hoey(?) for 27s.'
> 'Sold the grey bandy filley and grey colt to Jon. Knights (?)for a swap for £3 17 6.'

ABOVE Extract from photographed accounts of Thomas Acton relating to his father's death. Courtesy of the National Archives of Ireland (NAI), Business Records Survey (BRS), 2008/122/3/119/19.

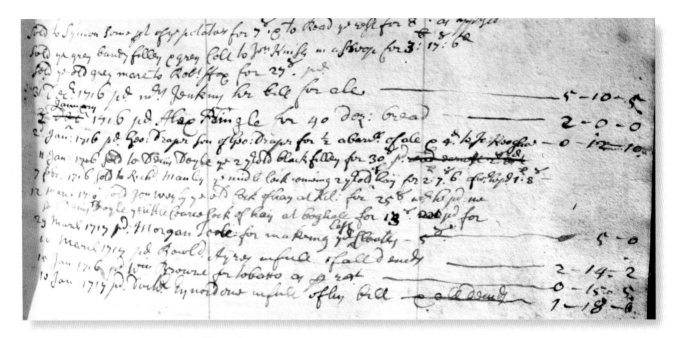

These agricultural transactions are mixed with domestic accounts settled for bread and barrels of ale:

> '31st Sept. 1716 Paid Mrs. Jenkins her bill for ale £5 10 5.'

Such meticulous farm records, written in a flowing hand, demonstrate an energetic, disciplined and punctilious mentality. Similar accounts relate to rents accruing from a dozen tenants of his own. Throughout the succeeding centuries this type of careful accounting was the norm, as the family records illustrate, and was probably the secret of their success.

The Dublin Society

One of the most practical and highly motivating influences on agricultural life and afforestation in particular in Ireland in the eighteenth and succeeding centuries was the Dublin Society (later known as the Royal Dublin Society). It was founded in 1731 by mainly Irish-born gentlemen of Anglo-Irish stock, many of whom were extensive landowners who were resolved to serve their country by land improvement and tree-planting. They introduced a premium system to encourage the planting of non-native trees such as beech, sycamore, chestnut, walnut and silver firs. In addition, they targeted different tree species from year to year, encouraging landowners to plant oak, ash, elm and chestnut; indeed, some towering specimens of these species, especially beech, sycamore, oak and silver fir, in Kilmacurragh date back to the eighteenth century. The records of the

Dublin Society cite the following statistic: 'The Society's land improvement and afforestation projects saw over 55 million trees planted in Ireland from 1766–1806'.[79]

An account from the 1730s details payment of £200 awarded to Thomas Acton for his invention of a 'dibbing' tree-planter. The same account shows that he purchased foreign timber for building purposes. In 1750 he received a premium of £10, again from the Dublin Society, which he spent on planting 'foreign' trees at the entrance to the Deer Park.

Thomas—an innovator

Thomas, characteristically innovative, was the first man in County Wicklow to grow turnips in accordance with the new *Horse-hoeing husbandry* of Jethro Tull, the Dublin edition of which was

BELOW One of the oldest yew trees (*Taxus baccata*) in the arboretum.

published in 1732, 'approved and recommended by the Dublin Society'. Turnips were grown as foodstuff for animals in Kilmacurragh (this too was a recommendation of the Society), and a field name—the 'turnip field'—survives from that time. Thus Thomas established a pattern for future generations of Actons who were innovators, invested in their lands and were good resident landlords, unlike those absentee landlords named and shamed by Thomas Prior, one of the founding members of the Dublin Society.[80]

Hundreds of yew trees

While the great number (over 300) and age of some of the many common yews in the garden are credibly remnants of the early monastic settlement—some yew groupings have suggested to Myles Reid[81] that they were grave-markers from that time—many were undoubtedly Thomas's additions. Those which now form the distinctive Monk's Walk, however, were planted as a hedge—then a popular demesne feature—along a presumed old pilgrims' path in the 1820s by his great-grandson, William Acton.

Thus started the Acton dynasty at Kilmacurragh, later known as 'Westaston Demesne'. It was a descendant, Thomas Acton IV (1826–1908), who opted for 'Kilmacurragh', an Anglicised version of the name from the middle of the nineteenth century. Perhaps this was an act of foresight, considering that in time Westaston Hill would no longer be part of the Acton demesne.

Sheriff of Wicklow

Thomas Acton of Kilmacurragh was an unpretentious, practical gentleman-farmer whose status in the community was reflected in the trust invested in him on his appointment to the important role of sheriff of Wicklow. This appointment was predicated on 'a substantial

RIGHT An old inclining oak, *Quercus robur*, on the lawn near the Double Borders at the back of the mansion, where some of the oldest trees in the arboretum grow.

income' and, *inter alia*, the 'duties of the conduct of elections for parliamentary representatives'.[82] He was an ambitious landowner, as 'within 30 years his family had moved from being minor landlords to 'the threshold of the gentry class'.[83]

Thomas's son, William, entered Trinity College in 1726—higher education was always a priority for the family—and acquired many prestigious titles there.

Thomas died in 1750, having established the ethical and commercial value of hard work and tree-planting on his estate. His meticulous documentation of farm expenditure and tenants' rents initiated practices which were to become the hallmarks of successive generations of Actons in Kilmacurragh. He was succeeded by his son William, one of his four children.

ABOVE Peony growing behind the mansion.

RIGHT Chinese wisteria (*Wisteria sinensis*) clings to a wall at the back of the mansion.

5

THE EIGHTEENTH AND EARLY NINETEENTH CENTURIES

William Acton (1711–79), keeper of the writs of the Court of Common Pleas, and his wife, Jane Parsons

William succeeded to the property on the death of his father in 1750. He had entered Trinity College in 1726, qualified as a barrister and rose to become keeper of the writs of the Court of Common Pleas. He was also a member, or sergeant, of the exclusive Order of the Coif, from which until 1839 all judges of the Court of Common Pleas were appointed.[84] He married Jane Parsons, granddaughter of Sir William Parsons, 2nd Bart, of Birr Castle, on 4 March 1736, and reference in the Kilmacurragh Book to 'the old high-backed chairs from Parsonstown' (Birr Castle) teases us into imagining other decorative additions that she would have made to the house, possibly echoing the décor of her family home in Birr.

During William and Jane's tenure the estate was further embellished with trees. To celebrate their wedding, a wonderfully romantic addition was made to the garden: a two-mile-long Beech

Avenue was planted in that year and splendid specimens of this tree type survive today, leading up to the Walled Garden built by his father in the 1740s. In the 1750s William had the business acumen to buy valuable woods in the Vale of Clara.

The Acton woods at Clara

The Acton woods at Clara supplied such wood-dependent industries as charcoal-burning ironworks and the many tanneries in County Wicklow dependent on stripped bark, which was more and more in demand at that time. As Eileen McCracken clarifies, the export of live cattle to England was prohibited, consequently boosting the demand for tanned hides from Ireland. The Dublin Society offered a premium of £10 in 1750 to those who tanned the most hides. The domestic supply of bark was inadequate to supply the local demand, with the result that, as Carey[85] writes, tons of it were imported from Scotland and Wales in the eighteenth century. Woodland business in general and bark production in particular were practised on estates close to Kilmacurragh, including the Meath estate near Rathdrum and the Croneybyrne estate owned by the Byrne family, which included several woods in the Vale of Clara. There were numerous tanneries in County Wicklow at that time—in Wicklow town as well as north of it in Ballinaclash, Croneybyrne (near Rathdrum) and Ballymoneen, west of Avoca village.[86] Timber was also closely connected with the increasing food-

LEFT One of William's splendid 'bridal beeches' (*Fagus sylvatica*).

exporting trade, which required casks and barrels for butter, salted beef, pork, tallow and fish to send off to the British colonies in North America.[87] A 'Valuation of the woods of Clara belonging to William Acton Esq.' dating from the 1750s included in the inventory thousands of barrels of both oak and 'birtch' bark, an indication of the scale and lucrative nature of the business. The total valuation of the timber stock amounted to £2,672 and 16 shillings.[88]

In 1762 William substantially altered the old stable-yard, first built in 1703, to create the present courtyard with its large coach-houses.

William and Jane's tenure was also very much influenced by the planting incentives of the Dublin Society. During the 1760s silver fir and spruce fir, Scots pine and Weymouth pine, larch, Norway maple, sweet chestnut and black cherries were added to the Society's tree promotion list.[89]

Both William and Jane responded to these incentives and were responsible for the planting of thousands of trees on the estate. By this time there were two lodges at opposite entrances to the demesne, one to the east and another to the north (towards Kilcandra), both of which still exist, though privately owned. In 1750 Jane received a premium of £10 from the Dublin Society for the planting of 'foreign trees' down by the lodge near the eastern entrance, and in the following decades trees were liberally planted according to the particular species being promoted by the Dublin Society in any given year.

TOP Japanese maple (*Acer japonica*).

ABOVE *Euphorbia* 'Amylassa' against the background of the Walled Garden.

OPPOSITE PAGE, TOP A corner of the coach-house yard serving as a little nursery area today. Thomas's son William substantially altered the old stable-yard, first built in 1703, to create the present courtyard with its large coach-houses.

OPPOSITE PAGE, BELOW This is one of four silver firs (*Abies alba*) which Samuel Hayes (c. 1743–95) brought to Kilmacurragh from his estate in nearby Avondale.

ABOVE The flower of the tulip tree (*Liriodendron tulipifera*). The tulip tree was brought to Europe from eastern North America by John Tradescant in 1650.

Thomas Acton III (d. 1817), high sheriff for County Wicklow (1781), and his wife, Sidney Davis

William and Jane's example of tree-planting was emulated by their successors. On William's death in 1779 he was succeeded by his son Thomas Acton III (d. 1817) and his wife, Sidney Davis, both of whom also earned premiums from the Dublin Society. In the 1780s the Dublin Society's list of recommended trees was extended to include, among others, scarlet maple, cedar of Lebanon and the tulip tree, a selection which influenced Sidney's tree-planting.

An entry in the Kilmacurragh Book refers to a Spanish chestnut that Sidney planted and also reports that she was responsible for the plantation near the lower, eastern lodge. This earned her a premium of £10 from the Dublin Society, with which she bought a red-flowering maple as well as an evergreen Grecian oak, among other ornamental trees.

'The plantation near the lower lodge was planted by Sidney Acton . . . and the Dublin

OPPOSITE PAGE Tulip tree (*Liriodendron tulipifera*).

ABOVE Autumn foliage of the tulip tree (*Liriodendron tulipifera*).

LEFT The ornamental red oak or northern red oak (*Quercus rubra*).
This is an exotic species which, however, grows well in Kilmacurragh. 'It is native to North America and has a broad range from Southern U.S. to Canada.'[90]

Society gave her £10.00 for it as a reward. With this money she bought the red-flowering maple and an evergreen Grecian oak etc.'[91]

This detail conjures up a portrait of a capable countrywoman actively involved in the business of stocking the demesne, something which is compatible with another record of her confronting the butler one night as he attempted to steal money from her room. His motivation may be explained, if not excused, by the fact that his wages were £2 a year and two pairs of white stockings!

The shaping of a landscape

Thomas received a premium of £6 from the Dublin Society in 1807 'for planting two Acres of Ground with Oak Trees in the County of Wicklow in the last year . . .':[92]

The fact that the wives of two successive heirs of the family estate planted trees and were awarded premiums also testifies to the family's interest in silviculture.

From 1784, as a result of monies expended in bounties and premiums by the Dublin Society, more and more acres were planted with trees in Ireland. Between 1766 and 1866 the number of trees planted through the efforts or initiatives of the Society exceeded 55 million and the total amount paid in premiums was £18,460 (about a quarter of a million pounds in 2013 terms). As Meenan and Clarke point out, 'the present day

RIGHT, TOP Old horse-chestnut tree *Aesculus hippocastanum* in the 'Fossil Lawn'.

RIGHT Darwin's barberry (*Berberis darwinii*) (Lobb introduced it in 1847).

> " RESOLVED,
>
> " That it is the opinion of this Committee, that *Thomas Acton, Esq.* is entitled to a Premium of £.6 for planting two Acres of Ground with Oak Trees in the County of *Wicklow*, in the laſt year, he giving the uſual ſecurity to the Society.

ABOVE Extract from the 1807 records of the Dublin Society.

landscape of Ireland reflects the planting of two centuries ago'.[93] Landlords like the successive generations of the Acton family who planted trees in their hundreds and encouraged their tenants to do likewise contributed to the wooded beauty of County Wicklow which we are privileged to enjoy today.

Agricultural progress in an unequal society

Parallel developments in agriculture were also fostered by the Society, with the aim of replacing expensive imports with home-grown raw materials. Some £50,000 worth of hops were imported each year for the making of beer, and the Society aimed to eliminate this need by encouraging the growing of hops in Ireland, just as they encouraged the growing of flax for the linen industry. They published papers giving instructions on malting, brewing and cider-making, as well as on the preparation of soil for the growing of flax. As progressive landowners the Actons engaged in all these activities, as the family accounts and outbuildings—including a brew-house, for example—and surviving field names like 'the bleaching field' bear witness. These and many other initiatives taken by the Society meant that by the end of the eighteenth century agriculture was in a prosperous state, culminating in the exportation of large quantities of corn (owing to the Corn Law of 1784 and the government's policy of non-intervention), beef, pork, butter and wool. This brought great wealth to the landowning producers, but the peasantry and labouring classes, mostly native Irish Catholics, were excluded from this prosperity because of high rents, high living costs, evictions and a growing population. They barely subsisted on a diet of potatoes and gruel. Many died of starvation during the famine of 1740–1. It is small wonder that such disparity generated frustration, growing discontent and serious political unrest.

ABOVE The wasted petals of *Rhododendron grande*.

The doomed rebellion of 1798—a Wicklow débâcle

The history of settlements or plantations throughout the country and the continual discrimination against the Irish Catholic population by a minority Protestant Ascendancy government meant that there was a constant threat of insurgency.

Just as in 1641, the sense of outrage at blatant injustice first found expression in Ulster. In 1798 a small group of liberal Protestant members of the ruling class in Belfast, in solidarity with the repressed Catholics and inspired by the American Revolutionary War (1775–83), founded the Society of United Irishmen. Their aims were to achieve reform and greater autonomy from Britain. The Society went underground and planned an armed insurrection with French aid. Before the call to rise reached the Wicklow insurgents in particular, intelligence reached the authorities; this led to the introduction of martial law in Wicklow, during which the militia inflicted brutal sanctions on suspects. These included torture, random floggings, house-burnings, transportations and other forms of state terrorism, which were also used to extract further intelligence. Graphic exhibitions in Wicklow Gaol,[94] where the insurgents were imprisoned, illustrate the inhumane treatment of prisoners characteristic of eighteenth-century jails in the British Isles. False rumours of rebel successes

ABOVE Fallen rhododendron petals and nature's detritus.

led to insecurity in the loyalist community, spurring the cavalry of Rathdrum, Wicklow town and Newtown Mount Kennedy to react in what was regarded as an 'exceptionally brutal' way. The insurgents' pikes were ultimately to prove no match for grape- and round shot, though *their* inhumane if sometimes effective stratagem of driving cattle in front of them during a raid often threw the cavalry into confusion. Ultimately, the lack of cohesion among the Wicklow rebels, the early arrest of their leaders in Wicklow and the indecisiveness of their colonel in Arklow doomed the Wicklow rebellion—and, historians would claim, that of the country as a whole.[95] After the defeat of the French fleet by government forces in the west, the outcome of the rebellion seemed inevitable.

Although Thomas and Sidney Acton were living in a staunchly loyalist district, as Protestant landlords they were fully aware of the danger to themselves and their family. Unsubstantiated reports of rebel victories and accompanying massacres led to a deep sense of insecurity in the Protestant community and thousands abandoned their homes. As a pertinent entry in the Kilmacurragh Book illustrates, Thomas was anxious to ensure the safety of his wife and children as well as of his tenants, and was acknowledged as a caring landlord in the local community. He offered the shelter of his yard to all the nearby Protestant farmers and their families.

> 'All the Protestant farmers living near brought their families to live in the yard where two fat oxen were killed for them to eat … In the year of the Rebellion [1798] Thomas Acton sent his wife and children for safety to Peter Street, Dublin. He and a friend William Maley in the Yeomanry remained at West Aston [Kilmacurragh]. On their way to Dublin, looking out of the carriage windows, the children were horrified to see dead bodies of rebels, but the sight became so frequent, that

at length it ceased to attract their notice. In order to make the house as secure as possible, the window frames were taken out, and filled with sods. A square of wood was cut out of the middle of the front door, in order to shoot the rebels from it.'[96]

Thomas Acton lost only one of his estate workers during the Rebellion—his wood ranger, John Bolton, who lived in Clara and whose task was to protect Colonel Acton's woods and coppices there. He was shot presumably because he took advantage of the absence of Catholics from their farms during the rebellion to steal their cattle and hide them in his employer's woods, making 'his own of them'.[97]

Other rather grisly details in the Kilmacurragh Book include references to the burial of a soldier which took place in front of the house near the sunken fence (ha-ha) at this time, and to a rebel who was hung between two ash trees in the quarry on the right of the dark lane, where his ghost is supposed to linger!

After the local rebels were quelled, they surrendered their pikes to Thomas Acton, a magistrate, laying them on the sweep in front of the mansion. Usually such surrenders required an oath of allegiance and the consequent pardon of the rebels. We do not know the precise terms, if any, agreed in this particular case. According to Ruan O'Donnell, however, clemency was used with some discretion, 'to diffuse tension in the area'.[98] He also writes that many of the United Irishmen in Wicklow 'remained in arms long after all vestiges of co-ordinated rebellion had disappeared elsewhere'.[99]

Such a policy of clemency was not universal, however. A chilling conversation recounted in the Kilmacurragh Book illustrates both the cruelly primitive punishments, such as pitch-capping, meted out to those who helped the rebels and the casual way such atrocities were regarded by the

ABOVE Dark clouds.

OPPOSITE PAGE
TOP A segment of the eighteenth-century
paddock wall, photographed in 2009.
It has since been refurbished, incorporating the
old stones with the new.

BOTTOM The refurbished old paddock wall (2014), incorporating
the stones of the eighteenth-century wall.

Ascendancy class whose magistrates had devised
them. The heads dipped in tar and speared on pikes
were, it seems, mere topographical reference points
for the aforementioned yeoman and family friend
William Maley, who had been out walking with
Thomas Acton and was temporarily disoriented.
Maley said: 'Oh! If I could only see the knobs, I
should know we were almost back again!' The
'knobs' were the heads of three men who had
aided the rebels.

A harsh judicial system

Such an attitude was at one with the harsh judicial
system presided over by magistrates of the
Ascendancy class, especially in the eighteenth
century. Hannigan reminds us that eighteenth-
century law enforcement was harsh in both Ireland
and Britain, especially in relation to crimes against
property. Punishments were often brutal and
disproportionate to the crimes committed. 'John
Fowler drew a life sentence for stealing a cow and
Jane Kelly got the same sentence for stealing a
lamb.'[100] In 1798 conditions were particularly harsh
in Wicklow Gaol (1702–1924). Insurgents (United
Irishmen) were either hanged or transported to
Australia. Accounts in the 1798 Rebellion Papers
archive[101] (National Archives), which should not
necessarily be taken at face value, refer to some
particularly ghoulish details that, in full view of the
inmates, a half-tame hawk fed on the decapitated

heads of executed prisoners as well as on prison vermin. Decapitated torsos were thrown into Wicklow Bay.[102] Other offences were punished by a catalogue of barbaric practices that included half-hanging, whipping, branding and the already mentioned pitch-capping. Prior to the 1760s, from which date some reforms had been gradually introduced, prisoners, including women and children, were kept in rat-infested cells, often shackled together or chained to the walls, with straw for bedding and no sanitary facilities.

Knowledge of these conditions puts all else into perspective and provides another dimension to the lives of the landowning gentry, whose position was becoming politically precarious but whose wealth cushioned them from stark reality by enabling them to focus on their special interests, including the collection of often expensive exotica for their pleasure gardens.

On Thomas's death in 1817 he was succeeded by his eldest son, Col. William Acton (1789–1854), high sheriff for County Wicklow in 1820 and MP for Wicklow in 1841–8. Given William's interest in exotic trees, many of which he purchased and planted in the demesne, as a preface to his profile it is appropriate to refer to the phenomenon of plant-hunting worldwide, which ran parallel to his life.

6

THE GREAT
NINETEENTH-CENTURY
PLANT-HUNTERS

A heroic generation: plant-hunters represented in Kilmacurragh

Colonial ambition, easier travel and missionary activity abroad led to more botanical expeditions in the nineteenth century and to the rise of a truly heroic generation of plant-hunters. These men performed feats of outstanding endurance, usually in inhospitable terrain, in search of plants hitherto unknown in the western world. Most plant-hunters shared certain characteristics: a precocious passion for botany, an eagerness to travel and a determination to master whatever they undertook to do.

Plant-hunters generally fell into four different categories. Some were professional botanists collecting for the Royal Horticultural Society, London,[103] or the Royal Botanic Institute of Glasgow or, like Joseph Hooker, for Kew Gardens. The Lobb brothers, Thomas and William, and Richard Pearce were employed by commercial nurseries, namely the Veitches of Cornwall. James Veitch & Sons of the Royal Exotic Nursery in Chelsea, London, sent out Ernest Henry Wilson. Others were missionaries, like Jesuits Abbé David and Père Jean Marie Delavay, who collected in Japan, China and Yunnan, while Augustine Henry was a medical doctor in the Chinese Custom Service who sent specimens of plants used in Chinese medicine to Kew Gardens.

All of these plant-hunters, as well as John Tradescant and George Forest, were represented in the collections at Kilmacurragh prior to the First

PREVIOUS PAGE Some of the exotic wild-sourced conifers on the Glade.

ABOVE RIGHT Oriental spruce (*Picea orientalis*). The tall oriental spruce (*Picea orientalis*), native to the Caucasus and eastern Turkey, is over 100 years old and stands to a height of over 30m.

RIGHT *Rhododendron rex* ssp. *fictolacteum* (Yunnan, Tibet and north-east Burma).

World War, when the estate was said to have 'the largest private plant collection on the island of Ireland' (O'Brien 2011).[104] These collections had taken the cumulative expertise of generations to develop. World War I took a heavy toll on the Acton family and their gardeners who served in the British army, and years of uncertainty followed, with inevitable losses from the collections. Those losses are being gradually repaired, as seedlings raised from recent expeditions to China and elsewhere have come to Kilmacurragh and now flourish there as young trees. These will take a century or so to mature but augur well for the future collections of the arboretum and gardens.

The passion for nature felt by plant-hunters is beautifully encapsulated in the oft-quoted words of Frank Kingdon-Ward, who made a prodigious 22 expeditions over 45 years for various sponsors:

> 'That was my night out: fireflies and bullfrogs . . . I just wanted to steep myself in an atmosphere, to revel in the scents, and to see with my own eyes all the exuberance of life, the warmth, humidity, and equinoctial time-sequence of the tropics.'

Because of the daring exploits of these plant-hunters there are plants from North and South America, Central America, Australia, Tasmania, New Zealand, China and Japan, as well as from Mediterranean countries, in Kilmacurragh arboretum. It is significant in human terms that these early expeditions lasted for three to four years, so the personal and social sacrifices were considerable.

PREVIOUS PAGE Species rhododendrons sourced in the wild by Sir Joseph Hooker contrast with exotic conifers at every turn of the many paths.

TOP RIGHT *Rhododendron arboreum* var. *roseum* (Hooker), Himalayas.

RIGHT Detail *R. arboreum* var. *roseum* (Hooker), Himalayas.

Of the many nineteenth-century plant-hunters represented in Kilmacurragh, perhaps two, namely William Lobb (1809–64) and Sir Joseph Hooker (1817–1911), have made the greatest impact on the heritage collections in the gardens in terms of the quality and number of plants they either sourced or introduced into Britain and Ireland. William Acton (1789–1854) and his heir, Thomas Acton (1826–1908), both avid plant-collectors and silviculturists, bought many of William Lobb's conifer finds in particular, and Thomas Acton, through his friendship with the Moores in Glasnevin, acquired for his arboretum the finest collection in Europe of (Sir) Joseph Hooker's rhododendrons sourced in the Himalayas.

William Lobb (1809–64), plant-hunter

'The singular success which rewarded his researches is, perhaps, unparalleled in the history of botanical discovery; the labours of David Douglas not even forming an exception.'[105]

With this fulsome praise the Cornish nurseryman James Veitch recorded authoritatively the contribution made by his employee William Lobb to world botany and horticulture. Lobb spent fourteen years actively collecting for Veitch Nurseries and his introductions to horticulture were numerous and important. At a domestic level, how many of us know that it was he who sourced in Brazil the many orchids we admire, including the swan orchid (*Cycnoches pentadactylon*), or the familiar passion flower (*Passiflora*), or the striking azure blue clitoria and a 'lobelia' (*Centropogon coccineus*) which grace our suburban gardens? He and Sir Joseph Hooker are the two plant-hunters whose plant finds and introductions account in large part for the historical heritage value, distinctive character and world importance of the Kilmacurragh arboretum.

Brothers William and Thomas Lobb were the first of many collectors to be sent out by the famous Exeter nursery business of James Veitch & Son. It was Thomas Lobb who recommended his brother William as a potential plant-hunter to James Veitch and, though William had no formal training, Veitch hired him in 1837, impressed by his natural facility for botany and by the quality of his collection of dried specimens of British plants. In addition, William had a strong desire to travel in order to discover unknown 'vegetation'.[106]

There was intense competition among

RIGHT The orange-bark myrtle (*Luma apiculata* syn. *Myrtus luma*) to the right.
Native to the cool, wet forests of Chile, this tree was discovered and introduced by William Lobb in 1844. It echoes the autumnal shades of the native beech hedge.

nurseries in the nineteenth century to be the first to introduce new, exotic plants to Britain. The exacting and commercially astute James Veitch entered the fray enthusiastically, deciding to send his own representatives to the Americas and to the Far East to source the novelty plants so much in demand for his wealthy landowning clients.

Veitch intuited that William had the precise qualities required for such a mission: he had devoted much of his leisure time to the study of botany, revealing a passion for the subject, and he was meticulous in his work practices. His reliability was later borne out both by his application to the task at hand and by his meticulous documentation of the plants which he had crated back to Veitch. His other qualities included dogged determination and the courage to face down danger, both amply exemplified in the course of his explorations. In addition, his docile nature and inexhaustible patience were his best shield in the trials to come.

He gladly accepted the proposal of James Veitch senior to go on a mission in 1840 to various parts of South America, where numerous physical and geographical challenges revealed his mettle and his extreme loyalty to his employer. During his exploration of the Orgaos Mountains in Brazil he collected some rare orchids, as well as *Passiflora actinia*, *Begonia coccinea* and countless other species which became favourites with Victorian gardeners.

Sometimes his shipments of cases of the plants, seeds and dried specimens that he had toiled to collect were destroyed owing to delays, negligence or the vagaries of the weather. In one trying instance of shoddy work practice in Panama, for example, the agent who was detailed by William to send cases of precious orchids to England failed to do so, with devastating effect. His laconic explanation was that the cases had quite escaped his notice. In that specific instance Veitch requested Lobb to replace everything that had been lost. Despite exhaustion and poor health, Lobb retraced his steps without complaint to recover the losses.

There was disappointment, too, when a consignment of plants contained few new discoveries.

ABOVE The brilliant colours of the peeling orange-bark myrtle (*Luma apiculata* syn. *Myrtus luma*). It has regenerated itself so freely in Kilmacurragh that it is rather like exotic scaffolding, its numerous luminous trunks 'supporting' the gardens.

OPPOSITE PAGE Chile pines—the popular monkey-puzzle trees (*Araucaria araucana*). Discovered in 1780 and introduced into England in 1798, the plant was made commercially available by William Lobb in 1843.

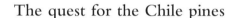

The quest for the Chile pines

From Argentina Lobb left for Chile by land, crossing the Great Pampas of the Argentine Republic and the Chilean Andes, where he travelled over deep, compacted snow, collapsing with fever several times. His main focus of interest in Chile was the great araucaria forests, where he had been required to collect seeds of the Chile pine (monkey-puzzle tree), *Araucaria araucana*, a species which Veitch considered to have great commercial potential. William and his porters made the laborious climb to a height of 5,250ft on the exposed ridges below the snow-capped volcanic peaks of the southern Andes. He devised an ingenious method of shooting cones from the trees, which spilled their nuts on the ground to be collected by the porters. He sent back over 3,000 seeds, and by 1843 Veitch was offering seedlings for sale at £10 per 100. This curiously shaped exotic tree was originally discovered in 1795 by Archibald Menzies, a surgeon on a ship visiting Valparaiso, Chile, who discreetly removed six seeds from his dessert at a banquet, which he later introduced into England.

After a couple of years spent collecting in

Peru, Ecuador and Panama, Lobb returned to England in 1844—much to Veitch's disappointment—but on recovering his health he was ready to embark on a second visit to South America. This time he discovered specimens of some of the finest trees in Kilmacurragh, some of them Lobb originals. From the Valdivian temperate rain forests of Chile Lobb brought back the dramatically beautiful Chilean firebush, *Embothrium coccineum*, the Chilean lantern tree, *Crinodendron hookerianum*, and the orange-bark myrtle tree, *Luma apiculata*, which has regenerated itself so freely in Kilmacurragh that it is rather like exotic scaffolding, its numerous luminous trunks 'supporting' the gardens.

Following these achievements, Lobb went to Chiloé Island, from where he introduced *Berberis darwinii*. This shrub, which had been discovered by Charles Darwin in 1835 during the voyage of HMS *Beagle*, thrives at Kilmacurragh, growing under a fine chestnut tree on the Fossil Lawn. In northern Patagonia he collected seeds and plants of the cypress *Libocedrus tetragona*, the Patagonian cypress (*Fitzroya patagonica*) and the cloud podocarp (*Podocarpus nubigenus*), which Veitch considered to be among the most interesting conifers, for England, that South America produces. Specimens of all of these conifers—there are seedlings of the venerable Patagonian cypress, toppled during the February 2014 storms—are thriving in Kilmacurragh.

Another rarity introduced by William Lobb that thrives in Kilmacurragh is Prince Albert's yew (*Saxegothaea conspicua*), a yellow-wood that was hunted in Chile and brought to Europe in 1847 for the Veitch nursery and named for Prince Albert, Queen Victoria's husband.

In 1848 William Lobb returned to England and was reunited with his brother for the first time in eight years, because Thomas had been collecting for Veitch in Malaysia and Indonesia.

ABOVE The honeysuckle-shaped bunches of orange-scarlet tubes of the Chilean firebush (*Embothrium coccineum*).
From the island of Chiloé, it was introduced by William Lobb in 1846.

ABOVE The holly-like spiny desfontainia (*Desfontainia spinosa*), which William Lobb discovered in northern Chile, gleams in the Walled Garden.

The 'messenger of the big tree'

By collecting large quantities of seeds of trees and shrubs which had already been discovered, William Lobb made it possible for them to be widely distributed, as was the case with 'the big tree'. It is by the moniker 'the messenger of the big tree' that William is most often remembered. In 1849 Veitch sent him to the cooler climate of North America in order to find conifers and hardy shrubs in Oregon, Nevada and California. William never once deviated from Veitch's strict instruction to focus exclusively on the collection of seeds, even ignoring the gold-rush in San Francisco at that time.

Lobb duly sent back seeds of various conifers, including the Monterey pine (*Pinus radiata*) and the ponderosa pine (*Pinus ponderosa*), specimens of which are in Kilmacurragh. William also collected sackfuls of seeds, cones and living material allegedly from a fallen specimen of the world's tallest tree, the Californian redwood (*Sequoiadendron giganteum*), which had been first introduced into Britain in 1843. The site of the 'big tree' had been rather naively disclosed to him by Dr Albert Kellogg in the California Academy of Science. Lobb quickly headed to the source, Calaveras Grove, where the dramatic impact of the enormous size of 80–90 specimens of this giant tree prompted him to coin the poetic description 'the monarch of the Californian forest'.[108] He took the earliest boat back to England, arriving in December 1853. A delighted Veitch raised the seedlings in commercial quantities.

That display of loyalty to his employer was to embroil William in a botanical controversy in 1853 in San Francisco. The Americans, with an acute sense of Lobb's 'betrayal', were outraged when John Linley, professor of Botany at the University of London, named the tree *Wellingtonia gigantea* in honour of the renowned British hero, the 1st duke of Wellington. Fortunately, this name proved invalid

ABOVE The Chilean yellow-wood Prince Albert's yew (*Saxegothaea conspicua*) (W. Lobb). This species was named for Prince Albert (1819–61), who was married to Queen Victoria. William Lobb brought it to Europe in 1847 for the nursery of Messrs Veitch.

OPPOSITE PAGE A Californian redwood, giant sequoia, Wellingtonia or Sierra redwood (*Sequoiadendron giganteum*). A species described by William Lobb as 'the monarch of the Californian forest' and which he introduced into England in 1853. There are a number of them in Kilmacurragh.

and the 'big tree' was definitively given its name in plant taxonomy by the American botanist John Theodore Buchholz (1888–1951). He named it *Sequoiadendron giganteum*, giant sequoia or Sierra redwood, justly commemorating the eighteenth-century Native American Sequoyah (1767–1843), inventor of the Cherokee alphabet or syllabary. In Britain, however, the tree is still known as the Wellingtonia.

Final years in obscurity

Whether that controversy accounted for William's lonely final days in San Francisco prior to his death we can only speculate. By the middle of 1854 William had been suffering from a complaint difficult to define, with symptoms described by Veitch as 'excitability and a lack of confidence'.[109] Nevertheless, despite some misgivings, James Veitch and his son decided to send William back to California with another three-year contract. In 1857 Veitch wrote to Sir William Hooker: 'We hear Lobb has been ill, his writing appears shaky and I am inclined to think it is probable he will soon return'.[110] Yet Lobb did not return to England but settled in San Francisco and continued to send back seeds to Veitch, as well as herbarium specimens to Sir William Hooker at Kew Gardens, something which rather annoyed Veitch.[111]

In time, the constant exposure to all weathers and the rigorous, often unreasonable demands made on him by Veitch took their toll. William last communicated with his family in 1860. By 1862 he was no longer active, having lost the use of his limbs through paralysis. He died in 1864.

The San Francisco daily *Alturas California News* for 5 May 1864 carries the only record of Lobb's death:

'In this city, May 3rd, William Lobb, a native of England, aged 59 years'.

<small>ABOVE Lenten roses (*Helleborus x hybridus*).</small>

Originally buried in a public plot with no mourners present, his remains were eventually removed first to South Ridge Lawn and then to a crypt at Cypress Lawn Memorial Park under the care of the California Academy of Sciences.

Sue Shephard's words in her history of the Veitch family are a fitting epitaph for this modest but heroic plant-hunter:

'William was arguably one of the finest but least-known of collectors who gave gardeners some of the most remarkable trees and loveliest plants ever grown'.[112]

Giving the conifers their freedom

A number of Lobb's finds and introductions from North and South America were purchased from Veitch by both William Acton and his son Thomas, both of whose lives overlapped with Lobb's. Though some are showing signs of age, many towering specimens of the giant Californian conifers, Chile pines (monkey-puzzle trees) and podocarps, to name a few, thrive in the spacious,

loamy arboretum at Kilmacurragh. Perhaps this is because they were planted according to a basic principle articulated by E.J. Baillie:[113]

> 'the true beauty and decorative character of the large conifers can only rightly be seen just in proportion as the trees themselves are allowed their freedom for development in the open and in natural positions'.

ABOVE The large conifers in Kilmacurragh were planted according to best principles, namely, 'allowed their freedom for development' on the Glade.

7

THE NINETEENTH CENTURY

Colonel William Acton, high sheriff for County Wicklow (1820), MP for Wicklow (1841–8), and his wife, Caroline Walker

On Thomas's death in 1817 his eldest son, Col. William Acton (1789–1854), high sheriff for County Wicklow in 1820 and MP for Wicklow in 1841–8, succeeded to the property. The Colonel was one of the most dynamic and colourful members of the Acton family. The following brief résumé of his activities, expressed in the continuous present tense, illustrates why: organising the closure of a local road, narrowing another to prevent undesirables from congregating, laying out the Rathnew–Arklow road for want of engineers, launching Famine aid projects, and all the while stocking the garden with exotic trees, earning premiums from the Dublin Society and serving as an MP. The sum of these activities give the measure of the man and his legacy to silviculture—a precious collection of heritage trees, many of them crucial for the perpetuation of their species.

Wicklow—a county of continuing contrasts

Wicklow was one of the better-off counties, with a strong and comparatively wealthy gentry. Of all counties outside Ulster, nineteenth-century Wicklow had the highest proportion of Protestant inhabitants, many of whom belonged to the congregation of Methodists.[114] William's daughter, Janet (1824–1906), was a keen follower of Wesley. The greatest concentration of Protestants in Wicklow was around the Acton estate, Westaston, where some townlands were 100% Protestant.[115] Many of the larger estates supported strong Protestant communities, usually situated close to the demesne lands. The Actons favoured Protestant tenants, domestic staff and farm labourers, who generally lived in Kilcandra, within easy reach of the demesne. Wicklow was a county of contrasts, where wealthy estates like that of the Actons, supporting their tenants, contrasted with the 28% of families of cottiers, labourers and smallholders (living in Redcross and Arklow, for example) who lived in one-roomed mud cabins. The staple diet of the poor labourers' families normally consisted of potatoes, milk, oatmeal and herrings, when these were available.

William married Caroline Walker, his first cousin, in 1818. They had seven children and, like their forebears, they had a great interest in silviculture and an appreciation for the beauty of nature, which they transmitted to their children. Keen planters of trees, they too were awarded premiums by the Dublin Society. As Myles Reid

OPPOSITE PAGE Budding oaks in a remnant of the old Coach Road (the Oak Avenue), closed by Col. William Acton, viewed from the stile.

recounts, 'William Acton received a certificate from the Wicklow Quarter Sessions of the Peace in 1821 for the planting of 15,000 larch, 15,000 Scots pines and 150 spruce trees'.[116]

As already indicated, William shines out from the family history as a very strong personality and a multi-talented man of action. His tenure was, however, overshadowed at a personal level by the family tragedies that he and his wife endured. Socially and politically, too, he was inevitably affected by the national tragedy of the Great Famine of the 1840s, during which he assumed his landlord responsibilities humanely and vigorously.

In 1818, soon after his marriage, William obtained legal authorisation to close the old coach road[117] from Dublin to Arklow/Wexford, which for security reasons had taken an inland route through Redcross, Rathdrum, Avondale and Newbridge (Avoca) that brought it close to his mansion in Kilmacurragh. According to local historian Ken Hannigan, this would have coincided with the opening of the 'flatter and shorter line of the new mail coach road' (the present N11). He imagines that 'once the new mail coach road had been opened William Acton would have been permitted to enclose the old road skirting his property. Leaving it open would have been an invitation to poachers and other trespassers.' William laid out

TOP LEFT Augustine Henry lilies, *Lilium henryi*, Double Borders.

MIDDLE LEFT A family passionate about silviculture: the tree collection behind the mansion, including the Mount Wellington peppermint tree (*Eucalyptus coccifera*), a Chile pine or monkey-puzzle (*Araucaria araucana*) and an Irish yew (*Taxus baccata*).

LEFT Old oaks, still stark in April, stud the boundary of the now-closed road.

the now-unused carriageway or 'lower avenue', merging it with part of the closed road, and planted it with alternating silver fir and monkey-puzzles, the latter introduced by William Lobb with such handsome commercial returns for Veitch & Son in 1853. Double wooden gates bar entry to this old carriageway, which has been under rehabilitation since 2013 and this year (2014) has been replanted with Chile-sourced monkey-puzzle trees, as well as seedlings from the original trees. It will eventually be reinstated as the main entry to the Botanic Gardens and Arboretum.

Mixed vintage oaks, believed to date from the late eighteenth century, still stud the boundary of the old road, guiding one's steps to its remnant, the unique 'Oak Avenue', where a continuous double-sided line of windswept, ageing hybrid oaks with wide-spreading crowns display the occasional limb whipped bare by the east wind. This avenue, in particular, is a vivid indicator of the passing seasons, as gaunt winter boles soften into spring freshness, then change to leafy summer foliage and finally blaze in autumn glory.

Though now grassed over, occasional old kerbstones push through to remind us of its former status. This remnant can still be accessed from the upper Barndarrig–Rathdrum Road by an eighteenth-century stone stile. In the eerie silence one can almost hear the creak of the laden carts as they lurched down the steep gradient on their way to make deliveries of timber and mining products to the nearby ports of Wicklow and Arklow. The colourful anecdote that Cromwell came this way after devastating the Catholic church in Glenealy may be mere imaginative speculation, although it lends an added *frisson* to walking along the Oak Avenue, especially in winter.

William and Caroline continued to develop the 5,381-acre demesne, as the 1838 OS map illustrates. Westaston, as the demesne was then known, is portrayed as being richly endowed with trees. Evident from the tree symbols in the map is

that in 1838 there was already an extensive amenity tree plantation close to the mansion and bordering the main carriageway. The 'bridal' beech trees planted by William's grandfather (also named William) for his bride, Jane Parsons, are also represented close to the mansion. This created woodland setting was characteristic of medium to large country houses at the time. The twentieth-century poet Austin Clarke's[118] line comes to mind: 'For the house of the planter is known by the trees'. Many fine tree specimens that form part of today's arboretum date from William's tenure. Also

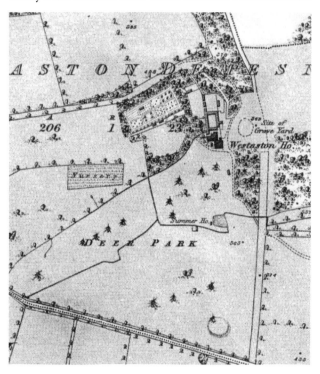

ABOVE A detail showing a close-up of Westaston demesne (Kilmacurragh).
Courtesy of the Map Library, Trinity College, Dublin.
Note the 'Site of Grave Yard' and the prehistoric monument indicated by a circle to the south of the Deer Park. It was William who removed these monuments. It is curious that the Dublin Society offered premiums for the plantation of raths. Note also the pond and summerhouse. A dotted line close to the 'Site of Grave Yard' traces the continuation of the coach road closed in 1818 by William Acton.

Top Common yews (*Taxus baccata*) frame the
Monk's Walk.
A lunging 'animal' lurks: the much-photographed
and climbed arboricultural curiosity, the 'rhino
yew'.

Left The 'rhino yew'.

depicted in the map is the nursery for propagation,
and the neatly and variously planted walled garden.

Michael Carey[119] refers to specific data for
County Wicklow which show that 'the area of
woodland in the county more than doubled
between 1791 and 1840 from 7,890 acres to
17,208' (William's tenure was from 1817 to 1854),
and Acton family documents testify to his
investment in tree-planting between 1820 and
1840. Clearly, William and Caroline left a rich tree
legacy which their son Thomas would continue to
extend to create the present arboretum. As well as
the monkey-puzzles and silver firs along the
carriageway, it was William who in the 1820s
planted the yew hedge, long overgrown, in what is
now known as 'the Monk's Walk', which forms a
nave-like corridor flanked by the double-sided
yews. These quasi-spectral yews lean angularly to
form 'natural sculptures', with one fearsome exhibit
carved out of a fallen yew by a former forester. This
lunging 'animal' is predictably a magnet for young
visitors! At the westernmost point of the walk
stands the oldest yew in the garden, believed to be
about 500 years old, its fluted columns folding in
the dark years with dignity and forbearance. It may
well have prompted the planting of the yew hedge.

William and Caroline had their own tree
nursery for propagation purposes (it was forbidden

ABOVE Mexican cypress (*Cupressus lusitanica*) or cedar of Goa. A Mexican tree brought to Europe in 1680 by Portuguese missionaries. Beside it stands the many-stemmed Lawson cypress (*Chamaecyparis lawsoniana* 'Cultivar') and the cloud podocarp (*Podocarpus nubigenus*).

RIGHT Another specimen of Mexican cypress (*Cupressus lusitanica*).

by law to remove saplings from woods) and also planted many exotic trees, sourced in the wild, which still stand today. Richard Pine writes that 'the planting of trees and rhododendrons had begun in Kilmacurragh as early as the 1820s'.[120] He is referring exclusively to exotic species which William's father had planted and for which he had received premiums from the Dublin Society.

As their dates illustrate, William Acton (1789–

1854) and William Lobb (1809–1864) were near contemporaries and it was typical of the ultra-modern Acton to want the most recent exotic finds in his tree collections, including some outstanding specimens sourced by William Lobb, the first of Veitch's plant-hunters. They were supplied by both Veitch & Son in Cornwall and Edward Hodgins, Dunganstown.

The Patagonian cypress, sourced by William Lobb (alas, one of the victims of the violent storm of February 2014), and the magnificent cedar of Goa, *Cupressus lusitanica*, supplied to Kilmacurragh by Edward Hodgins of the famous Dunganstown nursery nearby, were planted by William between 1820 and 1840. The cedar of Goa is still one of the most striking trees in the arboretum, and was the favourite tree of William's gifted son and heir, Thomas.

The commercial nurseries

As an ultra-modern landowner, William kept abreast of the latest findings of the many plant-hunters for which the nineteenth century was renowned. His main suppliers were the famous Veitch Nurseries in Cornwall, with whom the family would continue to deal into the next century. As we have already read, one of Veitch's earliest and most successful plant-hunters, William Lobb, sourced or introduced many of the heritage trees in Kilmacurragh. William Acton, like his father, also had the privilege of getting some of his supplies from the neighbouring nurseryman, Edward Hodgins, founder of the famous Dunganstown, Co. Wicklow, commercial nursery in 1780, in William's father's time. Over a span of three generations, at least, this prestigious nursery played an important role in the development of the arboretum at Kilmacurragh.

In 1786 and 1791 Edward Hodgins received premiums of £8 and £4 from the Dublin Society.

Describing Hodgins's conifers, the Scottish botanist J.C. Loudon[121] wrote that theirs was 'the best nursery collection'. In 1838 another Scot, Ninian Niven, described Hodgins as 'a most enthusiastic and successful cultivator who has done, perhaps more in Ireland, in the way of cultivating rare trees and shrubs than any other contemporary nursery…'.[122] He specialised in 'foreign trees and shrubs'. Among the specimen trees on his nursery was a cedar of Goa (*Cupressus lusitanica*), 54 years old in 1838. The iconic specimen of this species which stands proudly in the Glade in Kilmacurragh was supplied by Hodgins.

While William was a natural tree-collector, it was his son, Thomas, acknowledged as one of the most outstanding gardeners in Ireland of his time, who set about the actual creation of the arboretum as distinct from tree-planting—a very fine distinction indeed.[123] Undeniably, they were both in tune with eighteenth- and early nineteenth-century thinking among landowners who considered the arboretum and the 'pleasure ground', for both relaxation and stimulus, an

OPPOSITE PAGE Close-up of blossom of *Daphne bholua* 'Jacqueline Postill' shrub, Double Borders.

RIGHT With *Daphne bholua* 'Jacqueline Postill' to the left, recent plantings stud the lawn against a backdrop of some of the oldest exotic trees.

BELOW Western hemlock (*Tsuga heterophylla*). Native to western North America, it was discovered by David Douglas in 1826. This huge specimen, 30m high, is another champion tree for height and girth.

essential in the ideal estate. Their class had the wealth and leisure to travel and see exotic trees in their natural habitat before purchasing them from a commercial nursery to enhance their demesnes. William would appear to have been too busy to do this, but his son Thomas and daughter Janet had a very fruitful Grand Tour in the 1850s when they managed the estate.

The dates of purchase of the following trees sourced in the wild by Lobb coincide with William's tenure. Some of them are now deemed vulnerable and are on the Red Data List.[124]

Many of William's trees that are extant, some of which are Irish champions, are of heritage and conservation importance because they are known to have been sourced in the wild. Some of them are deemed 'vulnerable', i.e. under threat of extinction in their native habitats, according to the Red Data List.[125] Many of them, though vulnerable and producing non-viable seeds, are of great importance in terms of conservation—a process already under way, as evidenced by the many young specimens already planted out in their permanent positions in the gardens. Fortunately, a link to

ABOVE This Chilean lantern tree (*Crinodendron hookerianum*) was introduced from Chile by William Lobb in 1848.

ABOVE RIGHT A detail of the long, lantern-like crimson flowers of the Chilean lantern tree (*Crinodendron hookerianum*).

Kinsealy Research Centre has been made and a propagation programme initiated by Dr Gerry Douglas. A selective list of trees planted in the early 1800s, some of which are deemed 'vulnerable', includes the Irish champions Himalayan hemlock (*Tsuga dumosa*), native to the Himalayas and western China, and King William pine (*Athrotaxis selaginoides*), native to Tasmania. Other trees also believed to have been planted by William include Hartweg's pine (*Pinus hartwegii*); the drooping juniper (*Juniperus recurva*), a rare tree from the Himalayas, Burma and China, which was introduced in 1822; *Picconia excelsa* from the Canaries and Madeira, where it grows in the laurel woods; the Japanese red cedar (*Cryptomeria japonica*); and the champion Mexican cypress/cedar of Goa (*Cupressus lusitanica*) specimen by the lily pond.

These historic plants, which have withstood winter gales for almost 200 years in Kilmacurragh,

were seriously challenged in February 2014 and, as has already been mentioned, two precious specimens were lost. These old trees are in urgent need of propagation.

As well as the many trees sourced by William Lobb which William planted and spaced decoratively about the garden, there are other specimen trees sourced by plant-hunters Karl Theodor Hartweg, David Douglas and William Kerr from places as far-flung as China, Australia, Mexico and Tasmania.

Col. Acton, a man of action

William's breathtaking energy is illustrated by the following typical exploits:

'In 1820 the road to Kilcandra was very broad

LEFT Visitors relax in a sheltered alcove beside the Chinese fir (*Cunninghamia lanceolata* 'Glauca'). This is the finest Chinese fir 'Glauca' in Ireland or Britain. One of the world's most ancient types of vegetation (a similar plant being found as a fossil), it was discovered by William Kerr in China in 1804.

ABOVE Close-up detail of the Chinese fir (*Cunninghamia lanceolata*).

and cattle fairs were to be held there but William prevented this on account of the numbers of bad characters that frequent fairs … hence the narrow plantation of beech trees on (the) right side of the road beyond Kilcandra. In 1838 William levelled an area south of the main lawn with a view to laying out a tennis court. During this work a huge quantity of bones was unearthed. The area was the site of the pre-thirteenth century monastery graveyard. The unearthed bones were placed beneath a stone cairn near the fishpond below the house'.[126]

They remain respectfully cordoned off. Today a wildflower meadow has replaced the tennis court. The road from Rathnew to Arklow was laid out by William himself, there being no engineers in those days.

ABOVE The evergreen shrub Japanese star anise
(*Illicium anisatum*), introduced from Japan in 1790.
The branches are used to decorate Buddhist
graves, no doubt because of its aromatic leaves.

A family tragedy

Tragedy struck the Acton household in 1834, 1835 and 1841 with the deaths of three of the children, Caroline, Maria and Sidney. It was a period when infectious diseases were rife in the country. After the deaths of the three older girls, Richard Pine recounts, their mother Caroline 'refused to have music in the house, surely a severe loss for any child'. He also mentions the fact that the remaining siblings were almost entirely cut off from companionship with children their own age.[127]

One of their few close childhood friends was Fanny Alexander, the hymn-writer, who later recalled the girls and her youthful days at Kilmacurragh in a poem entitled *The Glistening Drops of Early Dew* (an extract from which is given below), which conjures up images of the nineteenth-century woodland garden and the joyful play of the children, their voices mingling with the hum of bees and birdsong:

> The glistening drops of early dew
> Lie late along the ancient park,
> And down the stately avenue
> The mingled shadows, long and dark

Of hoary beech and drooping lime,
Still linger as in olden time …

I tread your glades as in a dream
Of gleesome mirth in childhood's day,
And thronging all around me seem
Departed forms, and voices gay,
With lovely chant of forest bee
And wild bird mingles joyously.

Maria, those full eyes of thine,
Sweet Sidney's pure and placid brow
Thy laugh, light-hearted Caroline,
They rise, they ring to haunt me now;
'Twas but the tear that dimmed my eye,
The breeze that moaned, ye are not nigh.

The dark decade of famine and disease[128]

Besides William and Caroline's personal loss of three of their children in the space of seven years,

BELOW LEFT Crocuses for the lost children.

BELOW RIGHT Sunflower (*Helianthus annuus*).

the 1840s witnessed one of the most tragic events in Irish history, the Great Famine. Potatoes were the staple food of cottiers, labourers and smallholders, and each summer a 'temporary half-famine' occurred in the interim period when the old crop of potatoes had been eaten and the new crop was not yet ripe. It was then that families went out begging or ate weeds.[129] As early as 1824 a third of the population was already destitute. Successive failures of the potato crop and the collapse of the herring industry meant that there were food shortages in 1824, 1826 and 1827. Poverty, malnutrition and numerous evictions caused fever and mortality. The Poor Relief Act of 1838 was the first British response to Ireland's serious problems, obliging wealthy landowners to pay 'poor rates' to fund workhouses for the destitute. These were entitled to elect Poor Law guardians. Col. William Acton MP was the first ex officio chairman of the Board of Guardians of the Rathdrum workhouse in 1839, one of five set up in Wicklow. In what Eva O'Cathaoir describes as a 'sectarian age', officers of the first board were Protestant landlords while 'the inmates were overwhelmingly Catholic'.[130] Details of the shameful conditions in the Rathdrum workhouse over which Col. Acton presided as chairman make grim reading, provoking retrospective anger and indignation.

Col. Acton, 'the friend of the poor'

Despite these conditions, the perception of the local poor was that he was their friend. William Acton had the trust of the local people, as the following account illustrates:

'In Rathdrum there were two breweries. One of these was turned into a factory for making starch out of bad potatoes. The poor people fearing that their chief article of food was to be used for manufacturing purposes began to

ABOVE Pyrenean oak (*Quercus pyrenaica*), central and southern Spain.

raise a riot. The perception was that starch in potatoes could be removed and mixed with wheaten flour to make bread. However these experiments were unsuccessful.[131] Colonel Acton, a friend George Drought and some other gentlemen rode into Rathdrum to try and pacify the people. George Drought began to speak to them, but the people with one voice cried, "We will not hear you. Colonel Acton the friend of the poor is the only one we will listen to." He reassured them.'[132]

The shame of the workhouse

The workhouse in Rathdrum opened its doors to the destitute poor of Wicklow in 1841 and 1842. Referred to as 'paupers', the mostly Catholic inmates were issued with the workhouse uniform which displayed the Union's name, thus adding to the social stigma. The key workhouse officers tended to be Protestant and the ethos was a Protestant one. The workhouse was regarded as a last resort because of the inhumane, segregationist, anti-family regime there; no contact was permitted between married couples. A catalogue of the horrors of the conditions in the workhouse makes horrific reading: they were overcrowded, unhealthy (tuberculosis carriers were not isolated) and often violent; mental illness was not uncommon. Conditions had not improved some years later

ABOVE Horse chestnut tree (*Aesculus hippocastanum*).

when William's son, Thomas, was on the board. 'Unfit for human food' was how the medical officer for Rathdrum described the food there in 1899, no doubt because of the practice of buying in the cheapest provisions available. Many of the wretched poor preferred to commit an offence and be sent to gaol, where food was better, rather than stay there. 'The famine also copperfastened hatred

and shame of the workhouses in folk memory', recounts O'Cathaoir.[133]

A county of contrasts

Hannigan writes that 'In 1846–7 Famine made an unexpectedly early and devastating appearance in

Wicklow'.[134] Potato blight was detected by the tell-tale signs of blackened leaves hanging limply on their stems and a reeking odour filling the air. As the blight took hold and the herring industry failed, the poor were on the brink of starvation. The situation was further worsened by the rising price of foodstuffs.[135] It was an appalling injustice that people had to sell their meagre store of grain or pawn their fishing rods in order to pay their rents. Such inhumanity at a time when large quantities of prime-quality foodstuffs were being exported from Ireland raises serious moral questions.

The 'baneful habits of vagrancy'

The crisis of 1845–6 turned into a disaster in 1846–7, illustrated by some grim statistics[136] revealing that in the decade 1841–51 deaths in County Wicklow amounted to 16,930, a doubling of the normal death rate. Rathdrum workhouse expanded into the local brewery and the Flannel Hall, such was the demand for places, though 1847 reports describes them as 'in a state of disorder and filth'.[137] Besides malnutrition, people died of diseases such as fever and consumption associated with poor housing and a diet of diseased potatoes. While those discharged from the workhouses often died under hedges and by the wayside, a Rathdown guardian committee report of November 1849 listed 'those baneful habits of vagrancy and idleness to which many of the Irish peasantry were addicted'. Such were the blind, inhumane misconceptions of an unequal society.

Between 1851 and 1854 there were many emigrations assisted by landlords, including William Acton and his son Thomas, who managed the estate from 1851 owing to William's illness. Empty cabins were levelled and potato gardens were amalgamated into larger holdings. During the 1850s some 1,000 inmates of the Wicklow workhouses had been sent to North America as

ABOVE Flame of the forest (*Pieris forrestii*).

Poor Law emigrants, a preferred option to caring for them indefinitely in workhouses.

A caring parent

Famine relief works were set up by caring landlords, including Col. William Acton. His only surviving daughter, Janet, paid tribute in the family archive, the Kilmacurragh Book, to her father's generosity during the famine years: her 'dear father' was a caring parent, a benign landlord with a social conscience, evidenced by his humanitarian acts during the Great Famine times:

> 'Absentee landlords made it [famine] worse spending their currency in London instead of Ireland … The starving people came in multitudes to the eastern counties for help. About a 100 came here, our dear father gave them the great work of digging the fence round the Deer park.'

This work took about a year. William also hired famished workers from the west of Ireland to add two wings to the mansion as a famine relief project in 1848, the year he resigned his seat in Parliament.

A protracted illness

Colonel William Acton suffered a protracted illness, lasting five years. His son Thomas (1826–1908) managed the estate from 1851. William died in 1854, when Thomas formally inherited the estate. William's widow, Caroline, survived him for exactly a quarter of a century and died in 1879.

While Thomas is widely regarded as the chief moulder of the arboretum, we have both physical and documentary evidence of his father's passion for planting wild-sourced trees, and we ascribe Thomas's genius in part to his father's inspiration.

8

SIR JOSEPH DALTON HOOKER
(1817–1911)

(Sir) Joseph Dalton Hooker, unlike the self-made William Lobb, had a privileged background, a well-rounded education and a wide range of interests. Early in life he had the opportunity to gratify his great love for geographical botany. The privileged son of botanists, the grandson of an entomologist, a precocious collector of insects and mosses, he began, literally in petticoats, to grub walls in Glasgow for their hidden mossy treasure and to dream of a life of adventure in the footsteps of his

childhood hero, Captain Cook. His connection with Ireland began when he pursued his botanical interests in the west of the country as a young man.

Joseph Hooker's studies focused on the liberal arts and the natural sciences. He graduated MD in 1839 from Glasgow University and participated as a young man in the Antarctic voyage of discovery as assistant surgeon and naturalist to HMS *Erebus* in 1839–43. He spent four years exploring the southern oceans. His trips ashore enabled him to

Trees of *Rhododendron 'altaclerense'* and an Atlantic cedar (*Cedrus atlantica*) on the entrance driveway.

129

OPPOSITE PAGE *Rhododendron arboreum*
(Hooker).

ABOVE Burgeoning *Rhododendron grande*
(Himalayas, western China).
Seed of this species was introduced from
Tonglo and Sinchul, both near Darjeeling,
by Joseph Hooker in 1849. This specimen
was raised at Glasnevin from that Hooker
collection.

collect plants in relatively unexplored regions. A great systematist, he and Darwin became lifelong friends. Hooker classified most of the latter's plants and was his collaborator and sounding-board regarding his evolving theories on the origin of species.

Hooker's Himalayan expedition was undertaken in 1847–51, when he entered similarly uncharted territories. His plant-hunting journeys into the heart of the Himalayan mountains produced those very collections of rhododendrons for which Kilmacurragh eventually became most particularly famous. Before this expedition the conscientious young man had applied himself to a study of Himalayan and Tibetan geography and natural history. He was unprepared, however, for the massive scale of that territory: 'Upon what a gigantic scale does nature here operate!' he exclaimed, as he surveyed the steep, confused masses of the Himalayas.[138]

Hooker's objective in his Himalayan journey was to reach the snows. The greatest obstacle was the political situation and the difficulty in

TOP LEFT March blossom of *Rhododendron grande*.

MIDDLE LEFT *Rhododendron grande*.
This species grows wild in the Himalayas and was introduced from Tonglo and Sinchul, both near Darjeeling, by Joseph Hooker in 1849. The Kilmacurragh in-house tree notes state that this specimen was raised in Glasnevin from that collection. Its distorted shape indicates the strength of the westerlies that have continually assailed it.

LEFT Blooms of *Rhododendron grande*.

OPPOSITE PAGE *Rhododendron falconeri* in full bloom, its 'white dusters' blanched by the sun. This handsome tree was discovered by Joseph Hooker near Darjeeling in 1850. He named this species after Hugh Falconer, who was then superintendent of the Botanic Gardens in Calcutta. It has been described as 'one of the noblest' rhododendrons.[139]

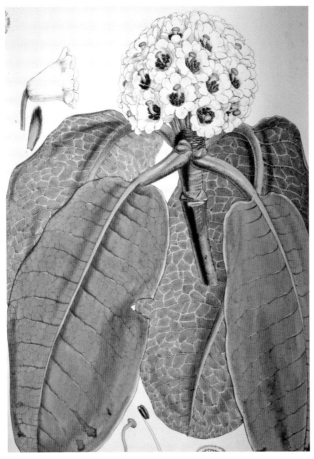

ABOVE *R. falconeri*, lithograph by Walter Hood
Fitch, botanical illustrator for Sir Joseph Hooker.
He prepared lithographs from Hooker's sketches
for his *Rhododendrons of Sikkim-Himalaya*.
Courtesy of the Library, NBG, Glasnevin, and the
OPW.

ABOVE *Rhododendron roylei*, Walter Hood Fitch,
botanical illustrator for Sir Joseph Hooker.
Courtesy of the Library, NBG, Glasnevin, and the
OPW.

procuring permission for a European to travel. He was the first European to collect plants in the Himalayas. He searched for flora in India and the Himalayas for three years, travelling arduously along the scorching plains over rough paths, plunging into deep, wooded (and often malarial) valleys and scaling precipitous mountain spurs to the snowy heights of the Himalayas, as high as 20,000ft. With superhuman courage and energy, he travelled by elephant and Tartar pony or walked for entire days; he crossed rivers in hollowed-out trunks or by minimal bamboo bridges. He even weathered imprisonment and starvation with

equanimity. He wrote to his mother, 'We [he and his fellow prisoner Dr Archibald Campbell] try not to make ourselves unhappy', demonstrating a quasi-oriental self-mastery instilled by his strict upbringing.

The breadth of his fields of research is clear from the numerous and varied instruments he brought with him: a barometer, a large knife and a digger for plants, a telescope, a compass and other instruments, a box for botanical samples, a thermometer, a sextant, papers for drying plants, measuring tapes, a geological hammer and bottles for insects.

At about 7,300ft he found rhododendrons, camellias, magnolias, hydrangeas and begonias; 8,000ft is the elevation at which the mean temperature most nearly coincides with that of London, i.e. 50°F. He thrilled to the 'noble plants' with their delicious scented blossoms: 'If I can only succeed in getting these glorious things to Kew, how happy I shall be', he recorded in his journal. Not only did they get to Kew but also to Kilmacurragh, via Glasnevin, into the safe hands of Thomas Acton. Joseph Hooker published his *Himalayan journals* in 1854.[140]

In that same year he was appointed assistant director to his father, Sir William Hooker, at Kew Gardens. In time Joseph succeeded his father as full director at Kew (1865), a post he held for twenty years. In the course of his tenure he successfully challenged with characteristic cool rationality an unscrupulous attack on his professionalism during the notorious Ayrton episode.[141]

Thomas Acton's trialling of the Hooker rhododendrons at the instigation of Dr David

Moore produced spectacular results: 'the rich blood crimson bells of Royle's Rhododendron as they hang in great clusters among its leathery leaves', the 'bouquet-like masses of *R. falconeri*', the moonlight effect of *R. triflorum*, the splendour of *R. kewense* x *R. thomsonii* and a host of others all figure in Hooker's *Rhododendrons of Sikkim-Himalaya*, a book 'which lies ready indoors for reference should any doubt as to specific identity arise in the garden'.[142]

One of the most beautiful trees in Kilmacurragh and which was also hunted by Hooker is the *Magnolia campbellii*. Planted in the Walled Garden, it pushes its brilliant pink blossoms over the wall in late February. Of the purple-flowered kind, Hooker wrote:

'It hardly occurs below 8,000ft and forms an immense, but very ugly black-barked sparingly branched tree, leafless in winter and also during the flowering season, when it puts forth from the ends of its branches great rose-purple, cup-shaped flowers, whose fleshy petals strew the ground'.

The rhododendron collection

The prestigious collection of Himalayan rhododendrons in Kilmacurragh were sourced in the wild by the Scottish botanical colossus (Sir) Joseph Hooker, curator/director of Kew Gardens (1865–85) and close friend of Charles Darwin (see above). Many famous visitors to the arboretum at Kilmacurragh enthused about the collection, including Frederick William Burbidge, curator of the Trinity College Botanic Gardens in Dublin (1879):

'The rhododendrons [in Kilmacurragh] would alone make the reputation of any one good garden, and they include one of the most complete series of the Sikkim and Bhutan and Nepalese species that is known. Nowhere else,

ABOVE *Rhododendron griffithianum*, a native of the Himalayas. First described by Griffith but introduced in 1850 by Joseph Hooker. The in-house tree-trial notes state that 'it is a very important rhododendron in the breeding of hybrids'.

OPPOSITE PAGE, TOP *Rhododendron barbatum*. Another Fitch lithograph from one of Joseph Hooker's illustrations. Courtesy of the Library, NBG, Glasnevin, and the OPW.

OPPOSITE PAGE, RIGHT *Rhododendron edgeworthii*. This was introduced into cultivation by Joseph Hooker in 1849. He collected it during his expedition in the forests of the Himalayas as he travelled through Sikkim.

not even in Devon or Cornwall, have we seen these Himalayan Rhododendrons so luxuriant in the open air.'[143]

Hooker's rhododendron collection came to Kilmacurragh through a series of fortuitous associations. His father, Sir William, director of the Royal Botanic Gardens, Kew, was in professional contact with Sir David Moore, director/curator of the Royal Botanic Gardens, Glasnevin, Dublin (1838–79), to whom he sent many of his son's Himalayan finds. Moore, in turn, was a great friend and botanical adviser of Thomas Acton of Kilmacurragh, to whom he brought many of these rhododendrons in the 1850s because the soil in Glasnevin was cold and alkaline and quite unsuitable for the calcifuge (chalk- and lime-hating) rhododendrons. Kilmacurragh, on the other hand, had ideal growing conditions for rhododendrons: a sheltered site, a granite and slate geological foundation and higher-than-average rainfall. In addition, Moore knew that Thomas Acton had a gift for nurturing tender plants. The rhododendrons indeed flourished and thus became Europe's most complete collection of rhododendrons from Sikkim, Bhutan and Nepal.

BELOW *Rhododendron arboreum.* var. *roseum*, a native of the Himalayas.

9

THE TWENTIETH CENTURY: THE GLORIOUS YEARS

Thomas Acton (1826–1908) and his sister, Janet Acton (1824–1906)

Rhododendrons, herons and dappled fauns— evocative images that feature in one of the most lyrical cameo descriptions of Kilmacurragh at a time when the gardens and arboretum were at the pinnacle of their beauty in the second half of the nineteenth century:

'Rhododendron Roylei gleaming above the tall grass below . . . in the tallest beech trees, the great grey herons are feeding young ones . . . To thus see the cool lush grass, and the flowers, and the noble trees against the sky, and to see the great herons wheeling slowly overhead laden with fish dinners for their nestlings, and to catch just one last glance at the dappled fawns and their young ones in the bracken, is to feel that "*Pan is not yet dead*".'[144]

Thomas Acton IV, William's eldest son, had been effectively managing West Aston from 1851, owing to his father William's declining health,[145] before legally inheriting the 5,500-acre estate in 1854.[146] His illustrious tenure would continue for over half a century until his death in 1908, in his 82nd year. During that time he and his sister Janet would make history as a dynamic gardening duo—

OPPOSITE PAGE Hiba (*Thujopsis dolabrata*). Brought from Japan in the 1850s, this tree has fourteen stems.

a fact acknowledged by visiting luminaries of the gardening world such as Frederick William Burbidge, William Jackson Bean and Augustine Henry,[147] who frequently made them and their arboretum the subject of their articles in horticultural publications such as the *Gardeners' Chronicle*.

'Mr Acton's garden is one of the richest furnished gardens in the country.'[148]

To describe Thomas's tenure as 'glorious' is not to exaggerate his contribution to Irish plant heritage. He was a passionate collector of exotica, as demonstrated in his copious garden diaries, where his lists of varieties of oaks and rhododendrons, for example, are breathtaking in their scope. His trialling technique, inspiring gardening practices, insistence on finding the optimum source for his plants and correspondence with learned institutions on botanical matters all add up to an extraordinary commitment to plant life and to the gentlest care of tender species. His arboretum in Kilmacurragh was like a beacon to plantsmen and writers such as William Robinson[149] who have immortalised him.

Childhood: a retiring nature

Thomas was one of seven children, of whom the three eldest daughters, Maria, Sidney and Caroline, had died prematurely in 1834, 1835 and 1841

ABOVE LEFT Cork oak: detail of a 100-year-old tree (*Quercus suber*). This evergreen tree is grown in Portugal and other Mediterranean countries. The bark has been harvested for thousands of years, its main use being the production of wine-bottle stoppers.

ABOVE Lawson's cypress (*Chamaecyparis lawsoniana*) near the Broad Walk.

LEFT Aromatic or Chilean laurel (*Laureopsis philippiana*). This Chilean tree has leathery leaves that are very aromatic and are used in South America to make a spice, Peruvian nutmeg or tepa. This specimen, planted by Thomas about 1868, is the biggest tree of its kind in these islands.

respectively, when Thomas was an impressionable eight to fifteen years of age. Consequently, he and the remaining three children had a rather sombre childhood.[150] They lacked the companionship of other children of their own age, and their grief-stricken mother emphatically refused to have music in the house after the deaths of her three older girls. Although their parents were caring and great lovers of nature, such stark isolation may have inhibited the children's personal development.[151] These circumstances probably accounted for Thomas's reserve, a lifelong personality trait even mentioned many years later in his obituary,[152] where he was described as being 'of a retiring nature' though also 'warmly welcoming to those who asked permission to visit the gardens'.

Janet's deep religious sense may also have stemmed from her lonely childhood. She was a 'devout Anglican', regularly attending two services each Sunday, one in the morning at St Kevin's Church, Dunganstown,[153] and the evening service taken by the rector of Dunganstown at Kilcandra in the hall of the schoolhouse. Thomas had built this school for the local Protestant children at his own expense in 1863. The last resident teacher there was a Miss Long. Successive rectors unsuccessfully appealed to him to have the schoolhouse consecrated as a church while still allowing it to be used as a school.

Janet was also a thoroughgoing royalist, illustrated by her enthusiastic celebrations on Queen Victoria's Jubilee Day, 21 June 1887, when

ABOVE RIGHT Hall's totara (*Podocarpus hallii*). Podocarps are an ancient family which flourished 150 million years ago. New Zealand. First described by the missionary William Colenso (1811–99) in 1844. He made many excursions with Joseph Hooker.

RIGHT A medley of species and hybrid rhododendrons.

ABOVE The Pyrenean oak (*Quercus pyrenaica*). Europe and north-western Africa.

LEFT A sample page from Thomas's garden diary, where he lists his stock of different varieties of oak.
Courtesy of the Library, NBG, Glasnevin, and the OPW.

LEFT White hellebore (*Veratrum album*), Double Borders.

BELOW LEFT Janet's favourite rhododendron, the cultivar *Rhododendron 'altaclerense'*.

BOTTOM LEFT Purple foxgloves (*Digitalis*), Double Borders.

she appeared oblivious to the possible counter-sensibilities of some of those attending the party.[154] Two years older than Thomas, she gardened with him until her death in 1906. They were devoted to each other and now lie buried together in the old Deer Park (currently a Coillte research nursery) under a favourite western yellow pine, *Pinus ponderosa*. This was a species which both of them had admired in its native habitat, Montana, during their Grand Tour and later planted in the arboretum in Kilmacurragh.

Family archivist

As well as being a keen gardener, Janet was also a meticulous chronicler of family events, including the demesne accounts, figuring such minutiae as the number of game bagged or deer shot in the course of the regular shooting parties at Kilmacurragh. She shared Thomas's enthusiasm for gardening and together they created what William Watson, curator of Kew Gardens, London,[155] described as 'the most interesting garden in Ireland'. Her outstanding extant legacy to the gardens is the Broad Walk, where her inspired planting provides some of the most iconic seasonal delights there, annually attracting faithful admirers.

Like Thomas, Janet was something of a trend-setter in gardening fashions, as her plantings of old roses demonstrated: 'Mr Acton's sister planted old roses about a sundial in the "enclosed" garden, anticipating Miss Jekyll's revival in this genre'.[156]

Polytunnels have replaced the old-fashioned roses but we do have a list of plants which were cultivated in the Walled Garden and which Thomas entered in his garden diary.

Indebted to her parents, William and Caroline, for her deep love of nature, Janet wrote tenderly about her father's planting of an orchard for his children because he himself didn't have fruit as a child.[157] Some hoary fruit trees in the Walled Garden may date from that time.

Education

Unlike his two younger brothers, William and Charles, who, in keeping with family tradition, went to military college, Thomas went to Emmanuel College, Cambridge, where he qualified with a doctorate in Law. After assuming responsibility for the family demesne he served as a justice of the peace and as high sheriff for County Wicklow, indicating his active involvement in Wicklow affairs. Thomas renamed the estate 'Kilmacurragh' *c.* 1860, using the Anglicised name of the townland.

The fact that Britain and Ireland have only three native conifers—juniper (*Juniperus communis*), Scots pine (*Pinus sylvestris*) and yew (*Taxus baccata*)—explains the desire of landowners like Thomas's forebears to import a greater variety of the species. It was thanks to their interest in silviculture and their enthusiastic response to the initiatives and premium scheme of the Dublin Society, active since 1731 (in his great-grandfather's time), that Thomas had inherited a legendary stock of non-native trees. These included oak, ash, beech, sycamore, giant silver firs, chestnut, walnut, larch and Norway spruce. One of the many visitors to the garden enthused:

'The giant sycamores here, with their dense green heads, are worth a long journey to see

...and there are some beech and ash boles that would delight a tree-painter ...'.[158]

In addition, Thomas's father William had kept abreast of the exotic finds of contemporary plant-hunters and added many of them to his collection, supplied by the famous nurseries of Veitch & Son in London and Cornwall and by the much-lauded nursery of Hodgins of Dunganstown, Co. Wicklow.

Thomas continued to follow his father's example by playing his part in 'the era of private planting in Ireland—the eighteen decades from the close of the 17th century to Gladstone's Land Acts (1881)'.[159] His personal style of gardening was distinctive.

'Man's actions perpetually bring him out of concealment, and he is then discovered, made to come close to us through his choices and aspirations.'[160]

This maxim, when applied to the 'retiring' Thomas Acton, is exciting in its revelations. His choice of trees, especially the great conifers, was based on his experience of seeing giant specimens in their natural habitat during his world tour. It was this privileged experience which created in him the desire to import them in order to inject fresh interest into an old demesne. Aljos Farjon[161] dubbed this typical nineteenth-century desire to import exotic conifers, in particular, the 'conifer craze', to which Thomas was patently not immune. He was able to indulge his passion for conifers in 1859–61, when, five years after inheriting the estate, he and Janet went on a world tour which lasted for over a year and which was influential in their transforming the demesne from a generously tree-stocked estate into an arboretum.

BELOW A riot of shapes and colours in the Double Borders.

OPPOSITE PAGE Scots pines (*Pinus sylvestris*) on the driveway.

The Grand Tour

The exotica sent back by the plant-hunters to the Royal Botanic Gardens and the big commercial nurseries in Britain led to the fashion of creating arboreta among the landowning class. World travel and the great Victorian pleasure trip, the Grand Tour, became an imperative.

Thus in 1859–61 Thomas and Janet Acton, with a view to 'clothing' their own estate with decorative exotic specimens, did the Grand Tour. They wished to research at first hand the conditions under which exotic trees and plants grew in their native, largely temperate habitats. During their fifteen-month voyage around the world they exhibited the same intrepid spirit of adventure as the plant-hunters, especially during their excursion on horseback through the snow-filled Yosemite Valley in California. Seeing the western yellow pines, *Pinus ponderosa*, in their native habitat, they resolved to grow them and many others in their own arboretum. Decades later, their final resting place, selected by Thomas, was beneath a favourite yellow pine in the eighteenth-century Deer Park in Kilmacurragh. This decision was made in the context of a rift with the rector of St Kevin's Church, Dunganstown, where many of their ancestors are buried.

Their tour also touched on the tropics—Hawaii, Fiji, Australia, Ceylon, Cairo and the Middle East. By the 1860s they had travelled the world and, as a result of what they had seen, they ordered many of the fine conifers on their return.

The conifers

Their fascination with conifers is understandable because, apart from their architectural stature, it is to these frequently wind-resistant trees that we turn for our real comfort in winter—to provide colour, like that of the blue-grey Atlantic cedar, or texture, such as the fern-like foliage of the cupressus and the cryptomerias. These trees continued to be readily available from those nurseries dating back to the eighteenth century, such as the Veitch nursery in Cornwall and the Hodgins nursery in nearby Dunganstown, which had supplied the demesne since their father's time. Both Thomas and his father, William, were among the first to grow William Lobb's new introductions.[162] Thomas knew that in order to appreciate the true beauty and decorative character of these large trees they must be allowed their freedom to develop in the open and in natural positions. This truth is illustrated countless times in the planting patterns employed at Kilmacurragh. Thomas's choices also reveal his ambition, taste and growing self-confidence. They bring him close to us. Indeed, trying to imagine Kilmacurragh *without* his trees makes us doubly aware of his work and vision.

Nevertheless, William Robinson, author of *The English flower garden* and a great admirer of Thomas, had a different point of view: he felt that the 'nobler evergreen trees' such as the Californian redwoods, while stately in their own country, 'marred the foregrounds of even fine old houses' in Britain.[163] He went so far as to assert that they were 'marring the beauty of the landscape and of our native trees'.[164] Undoubtedly, the questions of proportionality and type of terrain are crucial—considerations that make Kilmacurragh an ideal site for these noble evergreens. The semi-upland nature of Kilmacurragh (400–500ft) and the many other companion tall trees in the collection prevent any such unpleasant effect.

We experience an added dimension to our appreciation of the garden if we try to imagine Thomas's deliberations as he selected places in the demesne best suited to these great majestic presences, spire-like and erect, their trunks covered with fibrous, fire-resistant cinnamon-brown bark in the case of the Californian redwoods.[165] The glade leading down to the pond provided the ideal open space to showcase these giants, standing tall with towering Chilean monkey-puzzles, yellow-wood podocarps and Japanese red cedars, blending seamlessly with one of the four Hayes silver fir specimens brought from Avondale and the many ancient native yews. Thomas integrated his additions with his father's existing collection of both conifers and deciduous trees to form a noble arboretum which is a joy to visit.

'It is an old garden, its site is sheltered and fertile . . . the entrance gate, opening into a noble avenue of Silver Fir trees.' F.W. Burbidge further notes the cedar of Goa, *Cupressus lusitanica*, the fine timber trees, oak and ash, beech and sycamore, Scots pine and giant silver firs, with hawthorns and maples.[166]

In recognition of Thomas's scrupulous selectivity regarding the origin of his plants, Burbidge tell us that he acquired 'the best of all the productions of named suppliers from the best known nurseries of his time', such as the Royal Botanic Gardens, both in Glasnevin and in Kew, and the prestigious nurseries already mentioned—James Veitch & Sons, Coombe Wood Nursery, who importantly got their plant material from the original source through their plant-hunters, and the nearby Hodgins nursery in Dunganstown, which won many awards from the Dublin Society. In addition, Thomas was scrupulous regarding the status of a plant, whether it was a hybrid or otherwise, and kept records concerning provenance: a 'Moore plant', 'from Glasnevin', 'From Kew'.

The William Lobb trees

Following in his father's footsteps, Thomas bought several of William Lobb's discoveries and those of other plant-hunters from Veitch's Coombe Wood nursery. Ernest Harvey Wilson was their last hunter and plants raised from his expeditions to China for the Arnold Arboretum[167] were sent later to Kilmacurragh from the nursery at Glasnevin.

ABOVE Mexican cypress (*Cupressus lusitanica*) or cedar of Goa.

Richard Pearse, another of Veitch's employees, features in the collections. His find, the beautiful *Eucryphia glutinosa*, dating from 1859, grows just behind the mansion and is richly colourful in autumn.

Most prominent in the arboretum are William Lobb's South American and Californian plants, which he either sourced in the wild or introduced for commercial dissemination by his employers, Veitch & Son. These included massive specimens of the Chile pine or monkey-puzzle (*Araucaria araucana*), the Chilean lantern tree (*Crinodendron hookerianum*), the cloud podocarp (*Podocarpus nubigenus*), the orange-bark myrtle (*Luma apiculata* syn. *Myrtus luma*), Prince Albert's yew (*Saxegothaea conspicua*) and the Chilean firebush (*Embothrium coccineum*). During Thomas's time several trees were cultivated in the open air for the first time in

LEFT The curious twisting trunk of the Chilean or cloud podocarp (*Podocarpus nubigenus*), introduced by William Lobb in 1847.

ABOVE *Rhododendron arboreum* var. *roseum* (Hooker).

Britain and Ireland: the Californian carob tree (*Ceratonia siliqua*), the magnificent aromatic or Chilean laurel (*Laureliopsis philippiana*) from Chile, and *Nothofagus moorei*, one of the most beautiful of the southern beeches, which sadly doesn't grow in Kilmacurragh anymore.

Thomas's creation of an arboretum, though a fashionable thing to do, was not prompted by shallow vanity or by the contemporary Victorian desire to 'create the most impressive park' which, Farjon claims, motivated the new wealthy landowners in Britain, where an expanding empire

and the Industrial Revolution had widened horizons and generated 'idyllic views of nature'.[168] Farjon adds that old landscapes were altered and 'Artificial lakes, grottoes, viewing drives, and strategically and aesthetically placed plantations were created'. Thomas shared this awakening interest in reshaping his parklands. He had grown tired of the artificiality of the eighteenth-century Dutch style he had inherited, such as the ponds and the canals, and he put his own distinctive mark on the enlarged gardens, creating a sense of wild simplicity far removed from what William Robinson would have dubbed 'a stiff garden'. Today, from the moment we enter the driveway, we are aware of living things which have been planted with care and thoughtful consideration for distant effects. We enjoy the soft wildness achieved in the woodland copses, a backdrop to the specimen oaks and beeches, and the outer fringes of the lawns, which glow with seasonal colour—intense purples and saffron in spring, gentler hues of wild flowers in summer.

By contrast, Thomas's planting of exotic tree species was bold and painterly—enormous boles of redwoods and podocarps giving structure to the arboretum and framing clumps of wild-sourced rhododendrons, 'the most precious flowering shrubs ever raised by man', according to William Robinson. Thomas also cultivated a rich collection of Sir Joseph Hooker's Himalayan rhododendrons, many of which are extant.

A welcome distraction

A crucial external factor was also at play that caused Thomas, according to his great-nephew and heir, Charles Acton, 'to allow the land to deteriorate'[169]

and to indulge his absorbing interest in gardening and the creation of an arboretum. This was the worrying fact that agriculture had become depressed in the second half of the nineteenth century, owing to lower prices and competition from America. Later, the countrywide agitation for land reform would make the creation of an arboretum an even greater consolation and distraction.

Inspiring and productive friendships

The successful creation of the arboretum at Kilmacurragh owed much to the advice and collaboration of the world-famous 'pioneer of Irish field botany' Dr David Moore, director of the Royal Botanic Gardens,[170] and his son, (Sir) Frederick, with whom Thomas and Janet forged warm friendships.[171] Their professional advice and network of contacts were crucial to the evolution of the world-famous arboretum. After David Moore's death (1879), his son, 'Sir Freddie', as he was affectionately called, succeeded him as director and was also a much-loved friend and adviser to the family. During the remarkable combined father–son curatorship of 84 years the international reputation of the Botanic Gardens was firmly established. David Moore,[172] once assistant curator in the Trinity College Botanic Gardens, succeeded the famous Ninian Niven as curator of the Royal Botanic Gardens, Glasnevin, in 1838 and built on the foundations of both Niven and *his* predecessor, Wade. Niven had received generous donations from important English gardens such as Wentworth, Chatsworth and the Botanic Gardens at Sheffield. David Moore, too, in the course of his extensive travels throughout Europe, fostered connections with botanic gardens, nurseries and private estates,

LEFT Thomas's list, 28 March 1885, of plants received from Frederick Moore, Glasnevin. Courtesy of the Library, NBG, Glasnevin, and the OPW.

LEFT Artistic modification of *Rhododendron loderi* (Hooker).

were sent later from the nursery in Glasnevin. The Royal Botanic Gardens, Kew, became another of Thomas's major suppliers.

The Hooker connection

There were constant plant and seed exchanges between the Royal Botanic Gardens, Glasnevin, and Kew Gardens, London. As we read in the Hooker chapter, Sir William Hooker, director of Kew Gardens, exchanged rhododendron plants and seeds—sourced in the wild and collected during his Himalayan expedition by his son Joseph—with Sir David Moore. Moore, in turn, arranged with his close friend Thomas Acton in the 1850s to trial these rhododendrons in Kilmacurragh, whose virtually frost-free sheltered site, rich acidic soil on a granite and slate geological foundation, and higher-than-average rainfall suited these notorious calcifuges, intolerant of the cold, chalky soil in

with the result that he received many gifts of plants and seeds and the collection of rare plants in the Botanic Gardens, Glasnevin greatly increased. Through him Thomas Acton introduced many rarities into his garden and had the skills to succeed where many failed. There was a healthy reciprocity in plant exchange, too: Thomas Acton's garden diaries and the accessions records in Glasnevin illustrate the close ties and reciprocal exchanges of plants from the 1850s. Thomas's generosity in sharing the pleasures of his garden, and also his plants, accounts for his reputation as one of the outstanding gardeners of his time.

Thomas also purchased some finds discovered by Veitch's last plant-hunter, E.H. Wilson. Plants from his expeditions for the Arnold Arboretum

ABOVE An artistically modified *Rhododendron roylei* (Hooker), Sikkim-Himalaya.

RIGHT A list of rhododendrons from Kew in Thomas's garden diary, dated 1898.
By kind permission of the National Botanic Gardens and the Office of Public Works.

Glasnevin. This close collaborative relationship resulted in Kilmacurragh becoming a virtual annexe of the Botanic Gardens, Glasnevin, and in the formation of one of the most complete collections of Himalayan rhododendrons then known.

A triallist

Thomas's success in growing reputedly difficult or tender plants was due to his methodical and painstaking practice of trialling them. Whenever possible, he purchased three specimens of each variety and planted them in different places on the estate in order to test their individual requirements: where he thought they would thrive, where others thought they would do better and where everyone thought they would have little chance of survival. Some of his most audacious trials proved remarkably successful, like the monkey-puzzle trees

and rhododendrons which still stand out incongruously like defiant landmarks on top of Westaston Hill, which was part of the estate during Thomas's tenure. They can be enjoyed looking towards the hill on the Barndarrig–Rathdrum road. Given his form it is small wonder that Thomas's trialling of the Hooker rhododendrons met with spectacular results.

In 1867 David Moore could write to Joseph Hooker that he had seen eleven kinds of his (Hooker's) rhododendrons growing happily at Kilmacurragh, including *R. edgeworthii*, *R. wallichii* and *R. barbatum*.

An old list dated 31 March 1898 (see above), illustrating Thomas's vast knowledge of and

Glaucum

Grande

Kendricki

Keysii

Lanatum

Maddenii

Niveum

Roylii

Salignum

Setosum

Shependii   Bhotan Moore

Triflorum   Mangle

Thompsonii   Mangle

Hybrid of Thompsonii Mangle

Seedling from china Mangle

Wallichianum

Wightii

LEFT List of rhododendrons continued from Thomas's garden diary.
By kind permission of the National Botanic Gardens and the Office of Public Works.

BELOW LEFT *Rhododendron luteum* (Hooker).

BELOW A photograph of a page from Thomas's garden diaries, 1893.
The text reads: 'Protea cynaroides: I think may do under wall, keep him dry'; 'Magnolia Watsonia: I have set under North wall, same aspect as Cambellii'. Other plants are 'in the cool house'; there is a note to the effect that the 'frost kept out' and that the young leaves of an old plant of *Rhododendron dalhousie* are 'only woolly at edge of leaf. By kind permission of the National Botanic Gardens and the Office of Public Works.

ABOVE Early bloom of *Rhododendron arboreum* ssp. *delavayi*.

RIGHT *Rhododendron arboreum* ssp. *delavayi* now grows near the Monk's Walk.

passionate interest in numerous varieties of rhododendrons ('Barbatum 4 varieties'), is the true hallmark of a serious collector.

In addition, the lengths to which he would go to acquire, test, trial and nurture his plants was remarkable. His insistence on accuracy is illustrated in his correspondence with the *Gardeners' Chronicle* office in London, regarding the correct nomenclature for specimens that he had sent to them for identification.

Thomas's success with tender plants in the orangery, too, was renowned, and attributable to his acute sensibility and almost fatherly care towards them, as the page from his garden diary illustrates (reproduced left).

Thomas's skill in nurturing tender plants was typified by his success with the Chinese *Rhododendron arboreum* ssp. *delavayi*, which, together with *Rhododendron rex* ssp. *fictolacteum*, was 'raised

in 1884 by Maurice de Vilmorin in his nursery near Paris ... who then had plants sent to Kew and the duplicates were forwarded to Thomas Acton'. The deep, fresh loam on gravelly clay in Kilmacurragh and Thomas's skill coaxed *R. arboreum* ssp. *delavayi* to flower in 1904. 'It continues

LEFT Chinese gooseberry plants *Actinidia chinensis* from the Badong, Central China, collections are being trained into 200-year-old oaks bordering the new Chinese Garden.

BELOW LEFT *Aconitum carmichaelii* in the Double Borders.

BELOW Thomas's heated 'quaint lean-to green-houses' were built against this south-facing wall of the Walled Garden.
Note the hot-air vents in the wall. Wood fires were kept stoked by the garden boys.

to thrive and has recently been propagated.'[173]

A visitor to Kilmacurragh noted that Thomas was growing citrus fruits in his 'funny green houses'. He also cultivated bay, lemon, medlar, myrtle, orange, peach and walnut. Today, as an echo of that time, Chinese gooseberries originating in Badong are being trained into old oak trees— which once bordered the now-closed Coach Road—in the Chinese Garden.

Thomas's innovative work practice

Classic conditions for growing rhododendrons do not alone account for Thomas's success with the Hooker collection and other tender plants. His special personal qualities and work practices, together with his heated 'green houses' and the laying of a water conduit from a water source on

Westaston Hill to the house and garden, all played a major role in the success of his planting projects. Burbidge comments on 'the quaint lean-to greenhouses with their little panes and gables jutting up at different heights as they rise from one terrace to another'.[174] These were leaning against the warm south wall of the Walled Garden and were heated by wood fires which had to be replenished by the garden boys. Many rare tender plants were propagated here.

'Household god'

Both David and Frederick Moore enjoyed being house guests at Kilmacurragh and hunting those 'dappled fawns' in the Park. On the death of his father in 1879 Frederick Moore took up the role of garden adviser at Kilmacurragh. Charles Acton, Thomas's great-nephew, remembers that he was 'one of the family household gods when I was growing up … my memory of him is of infinite kindness and patience'. An amusing anecdote illustrates the warmth of his friendship with Thomas:

> 'Frederick Moore, who was a fine shot, once woke up in Kilmacurragh to find outside his bedroom door, in addition to the usual jug of hot water, a bottle of champagne with a note from Thomas asking him to drink the wine and then shoot a deer in the park so that they could enjoy venison the following week.'[175]

He was a great authority on horticulture and was free to travel widely in Europe, like his father, and was an expert in collecting plants. Collectors sent specimens from many parts of the world, especially China, Japan, India and America, so that the gardens in Glasnevin had to be reorganised and extended to accommodate them. Given the plant-exchange patterns between Thomas and 'Sir Freddie', many of these rare plants found their way to Kilmacurragh.

TOP Primula 'June Blake' in the Double Borders.

ABOVE Lawson's cypress (*Chamaecyparis lawsoniana*) (Oregon and California).

The Banks Medals—'most outstanding conifers in private ownership'

Such was the importance of the conifer collection in Kilmacurragh, a collection that he had partially inherited and further augmented with the help of 'Sir Freddie', that Thomas was awarded the prestigious Banks silver medal of the Royal Horticultural Society, London, in 1891 for the 'most outstanding conifers in private ownership.'

Sir Frederick continued to visit Kilmacurragh after Thomas's death in 1908 and advised the then heir, Thomas's great-nephew, Charles Ball-Acton (1914–99),[176] who lived in Kilmacurragh until its sale in 1944. In 1931 Sir Frederick was again instrumental in securing the award of a Banks medal, this time a bronze one, for Charles. In *Conifers in cultivation*, the report of the Conifer Conference held by the Royal Horticultural Society (London) on 10–12 November 1931, the point was made in connection with Kilmacurragh that 'all species of Coniferae do well here':

> 'Kilmacurragh possesses to an unusual degree the factors which make possible the growth of the more tender species. Its situation at a relatively high altitude near the sea, the northerly aspect, the form of the ground which is free from dips or pockets, reduces the possibility of frost damage to a minimum. It is well sheltered from the prevailing south-west wind both by rising ground and by tall trees on the windward side. The soil is a deep fresh loam: on the higher ground of an open porous

nature, on the lower parts damp and firm in texture, and is free from all traces of lime.'[177]

Some of the trees singled out in the report have succumbed to old age over the years, but many, including some planted by Thomas's father, William Acton, still stand nobly and were variously described as 'fine trees', or 'the fine ornamental tree' in the case of the King William pine (*Athrotaxis cupressoides laxifolia*).[178] The Mexican cypress or cedar of Goa (*Cupressus formosensis lusitanica*) was 'a fine tree', Prince Albert's yew (*Saxegothaea conspicua*) was 'a fine tree', while the Kashmir cypress (*Cupressus formosensis tortulosa* var. *cashmiriana* + *C. pendula*) was considered 'a beautiful tree'. All of these can still be enjoyed in Kilmacurragh today.

In recognition of the unique collection, the great Augustine Henry, the man who established Irish forestry, visited great Irish gardens, including Powerscourt and Kilmacurragh, with some of his students to show them the exotic trees there.[179]

Agrarian discontent

The political backdrop to Thomas's tenure included rumblings of agitation for land reform, which made him, as a Protestant landlord and a convinced unionist, the occasional target of Irish Republican Brotherhood 'hate mail'.[180] According to Charles, Thomas's great-nephew and heir, '... in his old age, ['old Tom'] probably became a bad landlord'. Such, however, was his devotion to trees and to the importance of forestry that 'he would reduce a tenant's rent for planting hedgerows or shelter-belt timber or for planting unusual species'.[181]

'Tom' was a realist and could envisage the eventual elimination of the landlord class and the erosion of rental income. Charles Stuart Parnell's support for land reform was misguided, according

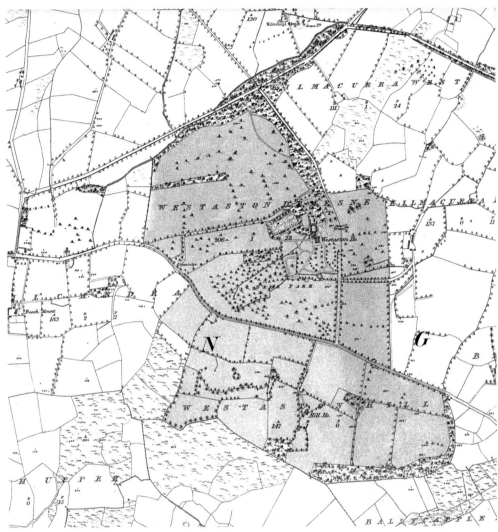

ABOVE Greater development of the garden, clearly defined paths and amenity tree-planting testify to Thomas's achievements.

to Thomas. Under Gladstone's Land Act (1881) tenants had a right to buy their lands, three-quarters of the money to be advanced by the Irish Land Commission. It aimed to make landlordism impossible. By 1876 the size of the estate had been reduced to 4,845 acres, and between then and 1913 the rental income had dropped to an all-time low. Friction between tenants and landlords ensued and Thomas bitterly accepted that radical political and social changes were inevitable. Nevertheless, despite these upheavals Kilmacurragh has survived today and is a fitting memorial to his work and vision.

The achievements of Thomas and Janet

Besides the bonanza of the Glasnevin Hooker collection of rhododendrons, the Kilmacurragh rhododendron stock included groups of the best hybrid kind, planted by Janet in the Broad Walk. Nevertheless, in his reply to an article by Jack Whaley in the *Irish Times* Charles made it clear that the wild-sourced material was the Actons' pride. Hybrids and cultivars were rare in the Kilmacurragh rhododendron collection—'they were looked down on'.[182]

The 1886 Ordnance Survey map of Wicklow, when compared with earlier maps, shows many of Thomas's achievements: we see a greater development of the garden, more paths marked, more tree cultivation, a pond, water tanks in the Walled Garden and glass-houses along its southern wall, and the former nursery area marked as planted without designation; the tumulus no longer features, and the site of the graveyard is still anachronistically indicated.

A decade later, the 1908/9 OS map shows enclosures to the east of the dwelling, many trees, the deer park, a large pond, a spring diverted to the garden, glass-houses, outhouses and enclosures. Ordnance field surveyors note the nursery, the deer park and the three-storey residence with extensive out-offices to the west.

Trend-setters

Both Janet and Thomas anticipated fashion trends in gardening styles.[183] Thomas's informal, natural style of gardening, described by the visiting William Watson, curator of Kew, as showing 'very little evidence of keep but there was much judgement in planting', was later an inspiration for William Robinson, whose name is now synonymous with the wild, romantic garden. The principles of Robinson's ideal garden correspond closely to the planting scheme practised by Thomas Acton and still observed by the present gardeners in Kilmacurragh: 'bulb and wildflower meadows, ferny glades with great clumps of rhododendrons, overlooked by exotic and native trees, surrounded by crowds of naturalised bulbs'.[184] F.W. Burbidge, like Robinson, delighted in the wild beauty of Thomas's garden. The Walled Garden also served as a nursery where Thomas and Janet propagated plants, gifting many of them to the Royal Botanic Gardens, Glasnevin.

Janet's Broad Walk

Besides being the family archivist, one of Janet's outstanding contributions to the arboretum was a classic Victorian feature called the Broad Walk, a popular feature which survives in some Irish gardens, including Fernhill, Ballinteer, Dublin. This walk is at the back of the mansion, separated from the Double Borders by a lawn planted with many of her father's old and precious trees.

The Broad Walk—so called because it was designed to accommodate the hooped crinolines of nineteenth-century ladies—is one of the characteristic attractions of the gardens, especially when the high-reaching rhododendrons '*altaclerense*' are in bloom in April, and shed their crimson petals all too soon—not dissimilar in effect

to the poppies of Flanders with all their tragic symbolism. The walk was planted by Janet herself in the 1870s, with alternating rows of the dark Irish yew (*Taxus baccata 'Fastigiata'*)[185] acting as a foil to the hybrid, crimson-flowered *Rhododendron 'altaclerense'*—which she layered herself—and the lower-growing *Rhododendron 'Cunningham's white'*.

The Double Borders

The great floral attraction in Kilmacurragh is a feature called the Double Borders, immediately accessible from the western side of the car park, where 'stepped' double herbaceous beds make August and September so memorably colourful. The policy there is mostly to grow flowers consistent with an old garden and in keeping with Victorian planting tradition, though some recently acquired exotica give variety and textural interest. During Thomas and Janet's time there were heated glass-houses here, backing onto the warm, south-west-facing wall of the enclosed garden.

F.W. Burbidge transports us to that era:

'The double borders … It lies on a gentle slope to the sun and drops down every now and then by terraces two or three steps at a time with its rare old roses. On one side is the wall of the great, square kitchen garden, and

OPPOSITE PAGE The plume poppy (*Macleaya cordata*) filtering the light in the Double Borders. Its native habitat is Changyang, in the mountains of central China.

BELOW The Double Borders: purple loosestrife (*Lythrum salicaria*).

against this wall are the quaint lean-to green-houses with their little panes and gables jutting up at different heights as they rise from one terrace up to another . . .'

Peeping into the green-houses, Bean sees the Cape gooseberry (*Physalis edulis*) heavily laden with fruit, orange trees and old scented pelargoniums—Thomas had great success with cuttings which struck root there in the delightful and unconventional green-houses. He cultivated citrus fruits and peaches in his glass-houses by the south wall of the walled garden.[186] He had the present pond constructed in 1894 for £60.[187]

George Nicholson, curator of Kew, was taken to visit Kilmacurragh and was particularly interested in the old orangery and the grapefruit varieties grown there. Other knowledgeable visitors who knew Kilmacurragh well were universally impressed with the quality and vigour of the garden's rare southern-hemisphere conifers and flowering trees.

Thomas Acton died in 1908 after almost six decades of managing the family estate. He was in his 83rd year and was unmarried. At the time of his death the demesne covered 600 acres. He was buried in the Deer Park beside Janet, as he instructed in his will, rather than in the family tomb in St Kevin's Church, Dunganstown.

The will

Thomas's will, witnessed by the carpenter Robert Wheatley and the wood ranger James Bolton, provides touching evidence of his care of his gardeners:

'I wish that £3 a year may be paid to each of the men in the garden as I have done every year . . . I desire that my body may be buried in the deer park near to *Pinus ponderosa* . . .'.[188]

Generous bequests to members of the Moore family further emphasise his esteem and affection for his close advisers on botanical matters.

The obituary

Thomas's obituary[189] appreciatively sums up his important contribution to horticulture. In particular, it refers to the many rare species of rhododendrons that he introduced, as well as rare trees and shrubs. His legendary method of trialling plants is mentioned. In the spirit of his own predilection for lists, important rhododendrons that he introduced are named: 'fine trees of *R. lacteum*, *R. delavayi*, *R. lanatum*, *R. shepardii*, *R. keysii*, *R. salignum*, *R. lepidotum*, *R. setosum*, *R. wightii*, *R. cinabarium* and *R. decorum*'. This list is like a sacred chant sung in his honour. Listed also are numerous splendid specimens of exotic trees in the collection, including the Chilean firebush (*Embothrium coccineum*), 'probably the largest specimen in the British Isles', and the wonderfully aromatic Chilean laurel (*Laureliopsis philipiana*). As then, 'many tree lovers from all parts spend an enjoyable time inspecting the gardens' today. Only the beauty of his vision remains.

A fitting tribute

It seems only fitting, too, that Thomas Acton, close friend and collaborator of the Moores, should have been commemorated in the creation of the hybrid *Rhododendron actonensis* (*R. actonii*)—a hybrid from *R. arboreum* crossed with *R. campanulatum*, white flowers spotted with crimson. Sir Frederick Moore wrote: 'it was raised by my father, named by me, a cross between R. *campanulatum* and white arboreum'.[190]

I am indebted to Mr Graham Hardy, Serials Librarian, Library, Royal Botanic Garden,

Top An April bloom in its fading glory of
Rhododendron actonensis.

Above *Rhododendron actonensis*: watercolour by
Lynn Stringer, 'Rhododendron "Thomas Acton"'
(by kind permission of the artist).

Above Wollemi pine, a gifted addition to the
Fossil Garden collection.
This pine was only known through fossil records
until the Australian species, *Wollemia nobilis*, was
discovered in 1994.

ABOVE Fallen petals of *Rhododendron 'altaclerense'*.

Edinburgh, for the following information:

> 'Rh. Actonensis is not listed in Fletcher, H.R. International Rhododendron Register, published by the RHS in 1958; however, it is listed in the second edition of the International Rhododendron Register, which was compiled by A.C. Leslie and published by the RHS in 2004. The entry is as follows:
> (r) "Actonii" cv. Parentage unknown. R: unknown (pre 1991) Fls. Creamy white. Tree-like form. May. Grown at Kilmacurragh, Co. Wicklow, Ireland.
> (r) = Rhododendron. cv = Cultivar.'

Postscript

On the centennial anniversary of Thomas's death, 9 June 2008, the current Acton family heir, Peter Acton, planted a *Quercus dalechampii* (similar to *Quercus petraea*, endemic to the south of Italy and which can reach monumental height) in the arboretum at Kilmacurragh. His wife, Sarah, planted a Wollemi pine in the Fossil Garden—a lovely gesture, ensuring continuity in their forebears' arboretum.

10

AFTER THOMAS

The grim toll of World War I—the Acton war heroes

As Thomas Acton died a bachelor and his two brothers, William and Charles, had predeceased him, he was succeeded by his nephew, Charles Annesley Acton, the 32-year-old son of his late brother Charles. Like his father and uncle, Charles had been educated at Rugby and the Royal Military College, Sandhurst, in 1895. He served in Malta, Crete, Hong Cong, India and Burma. When he succeeded to Kilmacurragh in 1908, Charles resigned his commission in the army and settled down to life as a gentleman farmer and magistrate, serving as both a JP and high sheriff for County Wicklow, as his uncle, Thomas, had done before him. His six-year tenure was interrupted by the outbreak of World War I in August 1914. He immediately applied for a commission in his old regiment and was posted to France. It is understood that many of the gardeners in Kilmacurragh also left for the front. Before the war eleven men and two boys maintained the grounds. The evidence of their sudden departure can still be seen in three cramped ginkgo trees in the Walled Garden, where as saplings they had been temporarily heeled in. No one returned to transplant them.

Tragically, a year later and in keeping with the distinguished army careers of his predecessors, Charles fell mortally wounded at the battle of Loos while helping a wounded man. Kilmacurragh then passed to Charles's only surviving brother, Major

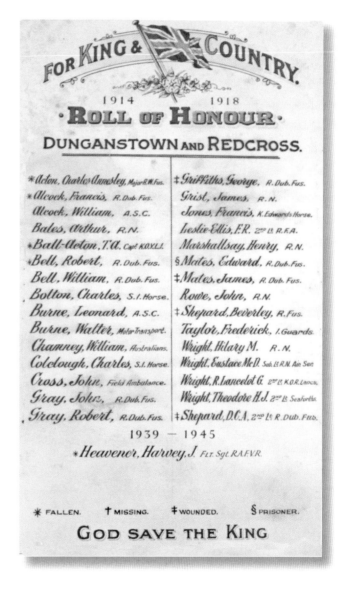

ABOVE Commemorative plaque for local casualties in the Great War, in St Kevin's Church, Dunganstown.
Note the two Acton war casualties: Major Charles Annesley Acton and Captain Reginald Thomas Annesley Ball-Acton.

LEFT 'Three gnarled specimen veterans in appearance' was how Jack Whaley[191] described the three cramped ginkgo trees still growing in their nursery positions in the Walled Garden.

These are believed by the staff to have been heeled in temporarily in the nursery area of the Walled Garden before the exodus of members of the Acton family and gardeners to the front in World War I. Included among those heroically fallen in battle were two Acton heirs, Major Charles Annesley Acton and Capt. Thomas Annesley Ball-Acton.

LEFT Budding crocuses for an infant heir.

OPPOSITE PAGE Work on making the mansion safe in 2009. According to Maurice Craig, the roof structure of Kilmacurragh was massive and apparently original.

Reginald Thomas Annesley Ball-Acton, also a graduate of Sandhurst. He had married Isabel Richmond in 1913 and they had a son, Charles, twelve months later. Reginald was killed in action at Ypres on 22 May 1916, barely eight months after his brother's death at Loos. Commenting retrospectively, Charles Acton said that the three lots of death duties imposed on the estate by the British government were financially crippling, something which his widowed mother bitterly resented, given that two Acton officers, namely her husband and her brother-in-law, had given their lives heroically for their country. She also thought that the meagre pension of £26 that she was given by the British government until Charles was sixteen was derisory. Nevertheless, she remained a staunch royalist, while at the same time being proud to have an Irish passport and apparently, in Charles's words, 'she taught him to be a republican'.[192] Quite a complex set of values!

An infant heir

The succession fell to the only remaining male Acton, Reginald's two-year-old son Charles.

Kilmacurragh had been bequeathed to his mother, Isabel, and in time it would become Charles's inheritance by deed of gift from his mother on his coming of age in 1939. Meanwhile he would continue his education in England.

The decline of the mansion probably dates from Reginald Thomas Annesley Ball-Acton's death in 1916.

The Queen Anne mansion that can no longer speak for itself

Visitors to Kilmacurragh note with disappointment the dereliction of Thomas Acton's Queen Anne mansion. Looking at its shell today, it requires quite a leap of the imagination to put flesh on its bones, both externally and internally. Culturally, its ruination represents a serious loss of both memory and texture of our past. All one can do now is prop it up to preserve some of its essence. While we lament what is irretrievably lost, there are fortunately, as we have seen in Chapter 4, photographs of the interior and exterior taken before its total decline, important references in any eventual restoration.

There were numerous attempts after 1944—when the property was sold—to save the mansion as it gradually fell into dereliction. Prestigious institutions, including the Georgian Society, expressed an interest and conducted exploratory examinations of the house. At the time the official opinion was that only the marble fireplaces and roof tiles were of any commercial value, and that, apart from the east façade, the mansion 'had no architectural features which would justify preservation'.[193] Since then, the building has been massively plundered of anything movable, including the marble fireplaces and beautifully ornate wooden door-case.

In 1976 Maurice Craig[194] observed that 'the roof structure [of Kilmacurragh] ... is massive and apparently original ... the oak remnants of the roof of the mansion . . . have survived almost three hundred years despite exposure to the elements for almost four decades'.

'A tortuous history'—a chronological account

After the death of two successive heirs, the estate and death duties were financially crippling. Charles's aunt, Irene, his mother Isabel and the latter's second husband, Hugh Digues La Touche, managed the estate as best they could, though in sum, to quote Richard Pine, 'the subsequent history of the house and gardens was a tortuous one'.[195]

Worth remembering as regards the architectural significance of the mansion is the fact that it exemplifies the design transition from the fortified dwelling house to the unfortified one.

1920s
The house in Kilmacurragh was abandoned during the 1920s and fell into disrepair.

1925
In 1925 Irene and Evelyn agreed in principle to rent the property at £100 a year.

1926
In a letter to the *Irish Times* in 1994, the late Charles Acton wrote that since 1926 his family had lobbied successive governments to make Kilmacurragh a branch of the National Botanic Gardens.

1927
By September 1927 the Hon. Lucy Phillimore, a novelist and friend of Lady Gregory, was renting Kilmacurragh on 'a seasonal basis'. Mrs Phillimore moved in with six maids and a chauffeur. She entertained literary and political luminaries such as W.B. Yeats and G.K. Chesterton, who stayed there. The Danish writer Signe Toksvig,[196] who lived nearby, visited frequently and recorded in her diary: 'Big old 18th cent. house, dismally gloomy, all furniture as if bought at third rate auctions ... but a garden like romance itself ... judicious neglect ... but superb prideful views ... Vegetation is noble. It owns the place.'

Years later, Toksvig would draw on her familiarity with the mansion and gardens in Kilmacurragh to describe the fictional Liskeen House and its parkland setting. She writes that Liskeen House 'lay in a large wild park, full of shadowing trees' which had the air of being the real masters of the estate. 'The house itself' she describes as being 'broodingly ugly'. Its interior had 'the dingy sadness and under-financed Victorian grandeur' characteristic of many country houses in Ireland at that time.

During the years after the Great War, the old head gardener alone kept a watchful eye on the precious tree collections for 40 years. Kilmacurragh archive records his pleadings to Lady Moore, with whom he kept in contact: 'Let yez come soon, the rosydandry falconyera or lowther is an admiration'. She responded and 'his verdict proved true'.

ABOVE April blossoms of *Rhododendron falconeri*.

In 1927, too, Isabel Ball-Acton, Charles's mother, who lived in England, wrote to her second husband, Hugh Digues La Touche, then acting as her agent in Kilmacurragh. Richard Pine records her reasons for not joining him there: '. . . I think of the dark house, the damp, the dirt and the discomfort of it—the big cold kitchen—and I feel sure that I would get depressed . . . I never worry about Kilmacurragh at all now—Kilmacurragh isn't the great black menace standing always at my elbow . . .'. Nevertheless, Hugh felt that it had become a millstone round her neck, since it was 'running at a loss'. He said that 'the mental atmosphere' there was 'a rotten and decaying one'. It has been acknowledged that the house had already fallen into disrepair. Hugh advised giving up the place.[197]

1930
By 1930 local and central taxation was taking £1,000. By then Kilmacurragh was rather a poor farm.

1931
The farm was sold off and the implements sold.

The Kilmacurragh Park Hotel (1932–42)

1932–9
Isabel's second husband, Hugh, was instrumental in leasing the property in 1932 to a Dublin hairdresser, an Irish citizen of German parentage: Charles Budina, 'citizen of Ireland. Hotel and agriculturist [*sic*] Irish table delicacies manufacturer. Tenant-occupier of Kilmacurragh 1st Sept 1932'.[198] Probably born in Germany, he was reared in Blackrock by an uncle and later worked as a hairdresser in Dublin. He ran Kilmacurragh House as the Kilmacurragh Park Hotel, in association with his brother Kurt, up to 1939, farming pigs and cows to produce delicatessen goods. Hugh commented that in Kilmacurragh there was life and work again and that it 'no longer looked derelict'. Budina built a ballroom at the rear of the house and set up chalets in the grounds for guests who enjoyed being close to nature. These have since been demolished. The late Maureen

ABOVE Mrs Maureen Gelletlie, late owner of Hunter's Hotel, Rathnew, Co. Wicklow, and one-time receptionist at the Kilmacurragh Park Hotel. Photograph courtesy of Hunter's Hotel.

THE MOST BEAUTIFULLY SITUATED HOTEL IN
THE GARDEN OF IRELAND

KILMACURRA PARK HOTEL

THE KILMACURRA PARK HOTEL, KILBRIDE, near
WICKLOW, stands amid lovely and extensive grounds, and is
an ideal rendezvous for Motorists as it is an easy run from
Dublin. Formerly a well-known Co. Wicklow residence, the
newly-opened Hotel is fortunate in possessing really wonderful
Park lands and gardens right in the heart of the most magnificent Wicklow scenery. The Parks contain the rarest
collections of conifers and rhododendrons in Western
Europe, and are for this reason visited by eminent
botanists from far and near for scientific
purposes. Here will be found all amenities
with the finest Continental cuisine at very
reasonable terms. Shooting, fishing,
tennis, bathing, riding and other
seasonable outdoor
attractions.

A TRIAL VISIT CORDIALLY INVITED

CHARLES BUDINA, PROPRIETOR

LEFT A southern view of the mansion was used in
this advertising leaflet.

BELOW LEFT Rhododendrons '*altaclerense*' and
'*Cunningham's white*' in the Broad Walk.

Gelletlie of Hunter's Hotel was a receptionist there
for a time. Budina, a Nazi, welcomed the Nazi
Party, who held functions at the Park Hotel.
Charles Budina returned to Germany at the
outbreak of the Second World War and John Finlay
writes that during a New Year's Eve radio broadcast
from Berlin in 1941 he sent greetings to his
family.[199]

Another brochure highlights an important
selling-point: the fact that the vegetables were
home-grown in the adjacent kitchen garden.

1939

On 26 September 1939 Charles Acton became the
owner of Kilmacurragh by deed of gift. He was 25
years old. At the same time he changed his name
by deed poll from Ball-Acton to Acton. The next
five years were crucial for Charles to find out what
his future should be. 'I hope it will not bring the
same misfortunes (to me) as to my predecessors.[200]
He took an interest in the farm and in the running
of the hotel.

The following observations give us an insight
into the status quo at the time:

> '... the grounds were magnificent. Every
> nationality stayed there. Dances on Saturdays
> and Sundays. In the (19)40s they built chalets
> out in the woods and you could have a room
> there instead of the main hotel ... It has a large
> variety of rare domestic and foreign trees.'[201]

In the '40s the demesne comprised 505 statute
acres, which included some fine agricultural land.

Charles came to Kilmacurragh as its owner. As
he surveyed his inheritance from Westaston Hill,

he thrilled to the fact that it was his, yet he felt that it was not so much his 'as a trust to hand on . . . to other human beings in distant times . . .'.[202]

1942

Budina left for the German front, leaving his large family in Kilmacurragh and placing the business in the hands of his accountant, Dermot O'Connor. Before his departure, Budina and O'Connor 'executed a deed of sale whereby O'Connor bought the business (leased from the Actons) for a nominal £100 from Budina, who also gave O'Connor power of attorney'.[203] This agreement was to cause great legal difficulties in the future. O'Connor felt morally responsible for Budina's wife and children, and appealed, unsuccessfully, to the German Legation to relieve him of this.

The sale of Kilmacurragh

1944

Charles Acton sold Kilmacurragh together with 400 acres for £4,000 (the optional purchase price on the lease) to Dermot O'Connor during Budina's absence.

Charles said that the mansion was 'simply dreadful' as a place to live and he had no sentimental memories of the house.[204] He went on to become an influential music critic for the *Irish Times* and played a major part in the fostering of classical music in Ireland.

Kilmacurragh—a national arboretum?

At this time it was proposed that the Kilmacurragh estate should be used as a site for a national arboretum, and the site was formally inspected in 1944 by a group including Mr de Valera (who was then Taoiseach), Dr Ryan (then Minister for Agriculture), Mr T. O'Connell (then secretary of

the Department) and Mr J. W. Besant (then keeper of the Botanic Gardens).

Unfortunately, because of lack of clarity regarding the legal ownership of the property, the Department could not proceed with the project.[205]

1945–70

Budina returned to Ireland in 1947 to find that Kilmacurragh had been sold and he was unable to buy it back. As his estranged family was living with Alfonso Palcic, he worked in Ireland until his death in 1954.[206] Budina's widow allegedly initiated a legal action in 1945 which was to last for almost 25 years.

After a protracted court case, Kilmacurragh was ultimately acquired by the Land Commission (1974). Two attempts at restoration ended in failure, one causing a fire that has destroyed more of the interior.

1969

Auction notice, Clarke, Delahunt, 10 April 1969:

'Kilmacurragh park on 405 acres, Distinctive part 17th cent. residence. The Auction description: spacious entrance hall, 4 reception rooms, domestic quarters, 7 bedrooms.'

Several attempts had been made down the years to have Kilmacurragh purchased by the state, something actively promoted by Sir Frederick Moore, for so long a friend and adviser of the Acton family. Such an outcome would also have been the fulfilment of Charles Acton's dream.

1974

The Land Commission purchased the estate, including the house, from Dermot O'Connor on 16 August 1974. The government handed over 100 acres, including the arboretum, to the Department of Fisheries and Forestry to be used as a forestry research station. It was later felt by locals that the mansion and arboretum (which were not part of

Coillte's brief) should have been given into the care of the Parks and Wildlife Service. The old Walled Garden became the administrative centre of the Forestry Research Unit and also housed a series of polythene tunnels in which experiments on seedling forest trees were monitored. The forestry officer in charge then was Mr John O'Driscoll. The departmental interest was exclusively in the development of the national tree stock. Today the remit of the OPW extends only to the gardens and arboretum, explains Paul Maher, curator, NBG Glasnevin and NBG Kilmacurragh, and does not include the ruined mansion. After the purchase by the Land Commission, the property was not open to the public because of the ongoing research project. A visit to the estate was by appointment only, as safeguards had to be maintained.

1975

From 1975 onwards Eric Joyce specialised in forestry nursery research at Kilmacurragh estate and held that position up to his death in 1983, an accident which saddened Charles Acton deeply.[207]

'The rooks' domain'

In 1976 Maurice Craig[208] observed that the mansion 'was falling down'. In her review of an Irish edition of this 'elegiac volume', published by Ashfield Press in 2006, Eileen Battersby[209] wrote that Craig saw a house as a statement and the 'death of a house' was always a strangely evocative occurrence. For him, she adds, 'every derelict residence retains its human relevance'.

1976

A report by the OPW stated the extent to which the building had already deteriorated.

1978–81

Once again the house was leased, as a summer residence for nuns and as a summer school.

TOP 'The mansion is now the rooks' domain, resounding with the ubiquitous, clamorous cawing of rooks.'[210]

1978

Kilmacurragh House was severely damaged by fire in 1978. Local hearsay refers to casual, unauthorised squatters in the house who lit fires in the attics, with devastating effects.

1983

Two attempts were made to try and preserve the house. The Georgian Society had expressed an interest in restoring it. To their secretary's letter of inquiry to the Department of Lands, National Parks and Monuments Branch, they received a reply (dated November 1983)[211] in which the expressed official assessment of the property was that only the marble fireplaces and roof tiles were of any commercial value, and that, apart from the east façade, the mansion 'had no architectural features which would justify preservation'. Since then, the building has been massively plundered of anything movable. The chimney blocks, slates, wall panelling and fireplaces went missing from the house during this period, as well as the marble fireplaces. The beautifully ornate door-case became detached and rotted away.[212]

1984

Jack Whaley, *Irish Times* correspondent,[213] urged the government to make strenuous efforts to stop the decline of Kilmacurragh.

1988

Bence-Jones[214] claimed that the house was by then derelict.

Appeals and castigations in national newspapers

1989

Many appeals for the saving of the house appeared in national newspapers, including one from environment correspondent Frank McDonald[215] in which he cites a hard-hitting editorial in *Apollo*, the international arts magazine (February 1989), on Ireland's poor record of caring for its heritage buildings. That issue of the magazine coincided with an exhibition at Christie's fine art auctioneer premises in London on the theme of the Vanishing Country Houses of Ireland, which documented the loss of over 500 'stately homes' since the turn of the century. The editorial made a plea for the establishment of a well-endowed national trust and appealed for an Irish acceptance of all aspects of its history—including, we infer, the architectural legacy of the Ascendancy class.[216] Indeed, an independent Irish trust, An Taisce, was founded in 1948, funded largely by members' subscriptions, but no appeals on behalf of Kilmacurragh are recorded in its archive. Today this trust has become the planning 'watchdog' of the nation. The OPW is the state authority currently responsible for Kilmacurragh Botanic Gardens. Its remit does not include the mansion.

1991

The government of the day was castigated for neglect of the mansion by Jack Whaley, *Irish Times*, 16 July 1991.

1992

Coillte, the state forestry company, put Kilmacurragh House, yard and grounds, totalling 51.6 acres, up for sale by tender. In April 1992 Bill Dolan of Wicklow bought the house—which was in a serious state of disrepair—and its site for an estimated £200,000–250,000, on the following conditions: (1) renovation of the house; (2) restoration and maintenance of the arboretum; (3) reasonable public access.

Bill Dolan estimated that restoration work on Kilmacurragh could cost £500,000. Kilmacurragh at this stage was described as a 'worthwhile conservation exercise' by Mr Christopher Southgate (specialist in conservation of historic buildings).[217]

1992

An article in the *Irish Times* Property Supplement[218] claimed that Bill Dolan, who had bought the property six months earlier, didn't have the finance to carry out the renovation. It reported that he hoped that local government organisations and the Irish Heritage Foundation could help. It was also reported that Kilmacurragh was visited frequently by local and overseas visitors.

The Kilmacurragh Action Group

Because the property was not open to the public at this time, Bill Dolan was opposed by protesters who had formed the Kilmacurragh Action Group. They were concerned at the sale of national assets by Coillte; they wanted public access restored and to have Kilmacurragh returned to public ownership.[219] They objected to the sale of Kilmacurragh to Mr Bill Dolan, who said that he too wanted the garden to be open to the public. Dolan claimed that the Group's argument was really with Coillte, whom Dolan defended, saying that 'it had done the best it could under the circumstances'.[220]

Kilmacurragh, one of the few Queen Anne-style country mansions, was on sale again after two years. It was in a ruinous condition, with most of the roof gone as well as the door-case and much of the interior.

Decline of the mansion

1996

After many years of slow decline, the Arboretum and Gardens were eventually bought back by the state in 1996.

In his piece on 'The story of Kilmacurragh', John Finlay (2011) alleges that the price paid by Bill Dolan was £180,000 and that the resale price to the state in 1996 was £240,000, when Kilmacurragh became part of the National Botanic Gardens of Ireland. The property was safe in state care under the Office of Public Works, who drew up a six-year plan which has been successfully implemented.

2007

The Irish Georgian Society suggests that a trio of houses in need of repair should be restored:[221] the Kilmacurragh mansion, Vernon Mount, Douglas, Co. Cork, and Hazelwood, Co. Sligo.

LEFT *Aster macrophyllus* 'Twilight', the Double Borders.

2010

The house was made safe in 2010. Its future depends on the availability of funds from government, to rebuild it.

2012

Public interest in the fate of the building has not abated. As recently as November 2012, architectural historian Peter Pearson[222] made yet another plea for 're-roofing the house and re-instating the windows', which would be 'an investment in the future'.

2014

My latest query (3 February 2014) to the Department of Arts, Heritage and the Gaeltacht regarding the future of the mansion was dealt with as follows:

'As you are aware, Kilmacurragh House is a protected structure under the care of the Office of Public Works. Kilmacurragh House remains an ongoing concern for the Office of Public Works and the Minister for Arts, Heritage and the Gaeltacht. Due to ongoing competing priorities, however, there are currently no plans to carry out works to the house.'[223]

If we accept that the slow decline of the mansion probably started in 1914, we must gloomily record that over the period of 100 years 'ongoing competing priorities' have repeatedly edged this heritage building towards imminent and irrecoverable ruination.

While today the almost completely restored arboretum and gardens are the obvious focus of one's interest and admiration, in order to 'read' them accurately one must acknowledge the primary role of the mansion, its site, style and orientation in determining the early garden design.

Imaginative proposals

In his thesis on the 'Kilmacurragh Arboretum Project' (2006), Myles Reid recounts what the former director of the National Botanic Gardens, Glasnevin, suggested as a possible solution for the derelict mansion: '. . . to make good the walls, cover the roof area with glass and use as an indoor conservatory and the wings repair for use as offices, auditoriums etc.'

Charles Declan Lyons, in his concluding remarks in his 'Building study on Kilmacurragh' (1990), claimed that the mansion, 'very much a rural dwelling', was worth saving. In contrast to the official view, Lyons saw many reasons why the mansion was worth conserving: it was one of only two mansions of a similar style in the country, it had been built on an earlier religious site, and it was linked historically to 'the plantation period' and other key episodes of Irish history. The unique timber door-case and surround, the traditional oak roof and the extensive interior timber panelling all illustrated the extent to which timber was used throughout the house. This was a significant fact, as at that time the property was 'in the hands of Coillte, the State Forestry Service, whose business was the planting and commercial use of native timbers'. The mansion, restored by master craftsmen, would have been a learning exercise for young participants and would have made an ideal research centre for Coillte, Lyons contended.

Practicable as these suggestions were in 1990, it must be remembered that neither Coillte's interest nor its responsibility included the mansion, which has deteriorated almost beyond recovery now. In 2014 one has a sense of optimism prompted by the wonderful achievements in the Arboretum and Botanic Gardens.

OVERLEAF A colourful salute from a beech on the avenue.

BIBLIOGRAPHY

Acton, J. [no date] The Kilmacurragh Book (Acton family archive). National Botanic Gardens, Dublin.

Baillie, E.J. 1898 The decorative character of conifers. *Proceedings of the Royal Horticultural Society*, 7 October 1898.

Bean, W.J. and Taylor, G. 1976 *Trees and shrubs hardy in the British Isles*. John Murray, London.

Bence-Jones, M. 1988 *A guide to Irish country houses* (rev. edn). Constable, London.

Bunbury, T. [no date] Acton of Kilmacurragh. Unpublished typescript. Available on-line at http://www.turtlebunbury.com/history/history_family/hist_family_acton.html.

Burbidge, F.W. 1903 In a Wicklow garden. *Flora and Sylva* 7.

Carey, M. 2009 *If trees could talk: Wicklow's trees and woodlands over four centuries*. National Council for Forest Research and Development.

Clarke, A. 1969 The Planter's Daughter. In A. Martin (ed.), *Soundings*. Gill and Macmillan, Dublin.

Craig, M. 1976 *Classic Irish houses of the middle size*. Architectural Press, London/Architectural Book Publishing Co., New York.

Cullen, L.M. 1994 Politics and rebellion: Wicklow in the 1790s. In K. Hannigan and W. Nolan (eds), *Wicklow: history and society*. Geography Publications, Dublin.

Donnelly, B. 1994 From Grand Jury to County Council: an overview of local administration in Wicklow 1605–1898. In K. Hannigan and W. Nolan (eds), *Wicklow: history and society*. Geography Publications, Dublin.

Doyle, J. 1963 *The place of a national arboretum in the Irish economy*. Royal Dublin Society, Dublin.

Farjon, A. 2008 *A natural history of conifers*. Timber Press, Portland, Oregon.

Finlay, J. 2011 The story of Kilmacurragh. *Wicklow Historical Society Journal* 4 (3).

Hannigan, K. 1994 Wicklow before and after the Famine. In K. Hannigan and W. Nolan (eds), *Wicklow: history and society*. Geography Publications, Dublin.

Hannigan, K. and Nolan, W. (eds) 1994 *Wicklow: history and society*. Geography Publications, Dublin.

Hayes, S. 1794 *A practical treatise on planting and the management of woods and coppices*. Royal Dublin Society, Dublin.

Heavener, R. 1993 *Credo*. Cromlech Books, Jordanstown.

Hooker, J.D. 1849–51 *The rhododendrons of Sikkim-Himalaya* (ed. Sir W.J. Hooker). Reeve, Benham and Reeve, London.

Hooker, J.D. 1854 *Himalayan journals; or, Notes of a naturalist, in Bengal, the Sikkim and Nepal Himalayas, Khasia Mountains &c.* John Murray, London.

Huxley, L. 1918 *Life and letters of Sir Joseph Dalton Hooker, O.M., G.C.S.I.: based on materials collected and arranged by Lady Hooker*. John Murray, London.

Loeber, R. 1994 Settlers' utilisation of the natural resources. In K. Hannigan and W. Nolan (eds), *Wicklow: history and society*. Geography Publications, Dublin.

Lyons, C.D. 1990 Building study on Kilmacurragh. Institute of Architects of Ireland Archive, Dublin.

McCracken, E. 1971 *The Irish woods since Tudor times, their distribution and exploitation*. David and Charles,

Newton Abbot.

Malins, E. and Bowe, P. 1980 *Irish gardens and demesnes from 1830*. Barrie and Jenkins, London.

Meenan, T. and Clarke, D. (eds) 1981 *The Royal Dublin Society*. Gill and Macmillan, Dublin.

Moody, T.W. and Martin, F.X. (eds) 1967 *The course of Irish history*. The Mercier Press, Cork.

O'Brien, S. 2008 Thomas Acton, a centennial celebration at Kilmacurragh. *Newsletter of the Irish Garden Plant Society* **109** (July 2008).

O'Brien, S. 2011 *In the footsteps of Augustine Henry and his Chinese plant collectors*. Garden Art Press, Woodbridge.

O'Cathaoir, E. 1994 The Poor Law in County Wicklow. In K. Hannigan and W. Nolan (eds), *Wicklow: history and society*. Geography Publications, Dublin.

O'Donnell, R. (ed.) 1988 *Insurgent Wicklow, 1798: the story as written by Luke Cullen*. Kestrel Books, Wicklow.

O'Donnell, R. 1994 The rebellion of 1798 in County Wicklow. In K. Hannigan and W. Nolan (eds), *Wicklow: history and society*. Geography Publications, Dublin.

O'Hanlon, J. 1873 *Lives of the Irish saints*. James Duffy and Sons, Dublin/Burns, Oats and Co., London/The Catholic Publishing Society, New York.

O'Riain, P. 2011 *A dictionary of Irish saints*. Four Courts Press, Dublin.

Pearson, P. 2012 From the ashes. *Irish Arts Review* (September–November 2012).

Peill, J. and the Knight of Glin 2007 *Irish furniture: woodwork and carving from the earliest times to the Act of Union*. Yale University Press, New Haven and London.

Pihl, L. (ed.) 1994 *Signe Toksvig's Irish diaries 1926–1937*. Lilliput Press, Dublin.

Pine, L.G. (ed.) 1958 *Burke's genealogical heraldic history of the landed gentry of Ireland* (4th edn). London.

Pine, R. 2010 *Charles: the life and world of Charles Acton 1914–1999*. The Lilliput Press, Dublin.

Plummer, C. 1910 *Vitae sanctorum Hiberniae* (2 vols). Oxford.

Price, L. 1945–67 *The place-names of County Wicklow* (7 vols). [Reprinted by the Dublin Institute for Advanced Studies, Dublin.]

Reid, M. 2006 Kilmacurragh Arboretum Project. Unpublished thesis for BSc. in Agriculture. National Botanic Gardens, Dublin.

Robinson, W. 1901 *The English flower garden, and home grounds*. John Murray, London.

Rutherford, J. 1992 *Country house lighting, 1660–1890*. Leeds City Art Galleries, Leeds.

Shephard, S. 2003 *Seeds of fortune—a gardening dynasty*. Bloomsbury Publishing, London.

Thistleton-Dyer, W.T. 1906 Preface. In H.J. Elwes and A. Henry, *The trees of Gt Britain and Ireland* (7 vols) (Edinburgh, 1906–13). Facsimile reprinted by the Society of Irish Foresters, 2012.

Toksvig, S. 1935 *Eve's doctor*. Faber and Faber, London.

Veitch, J.H. 1900 *A manual of Coniferae* (2nd edn). Veitch, London.

Veitch, J.H. 1906 *Hortus Veitchii: a history of the rise and progress of the nurseries of Messrs James Veitch and Sons*. Veitch, London.

Viney, M. 2003 *Ireland—a Smithsonian natural history*. Blackstaff Press, Belfast.

NOTES

1   From E.J. Baillie, 'The decorative character of conifers'.
2   Notes from a conversation with Paul Norton, 30 April 1998, courtesy of Jane Powers.
3   Matthew Jebb, Director, National Botanic Gardens, Glasnevin, Dublin, pers. comm.
4   Matthew Jebb, Director, National Botanic Gardens, pers. comm.
5   I am indebted to Matthew Jebb, Director, NBG, for this information.
6   Take the junction to the right either at the Beehive pub, Kilbride, or 3–4km further south at the Tap Bar and Café and follow the signs for Kilmacurra. As I write, the N11 is undergoing restructuring, so access points may change.
7   This list of shrubs was supplied by Paul Maher, curator, National Botanic Gardens, Glasnevin and Kilmacurragh.
8   Thistleton-Dyer 1906. William Turner Thistleton-Dyer, botanist, was director of the Royal Botanic Gardens, Kew.
9   Courtesy of the Royal Horticultural Society, Vincent Square, London.
10 Pihl 1994, 108.
11 Letters, *Irish Times*, 14 May 1984.
12 Coillte (meaning 'woods/forest') is a state-sponsored company in Ireland, established on 8 December 1988 and owned by the Irish government. Kilmacurragh was initially bought in 1975 by the government, who handed over 100 acres, including the arboretum, to the Department of Fisheries and Forestry (renamed Coillte) to be used as a forestry research station.
13 Matthew Jebb, NBG, Glasnevin.
14 O'Brien 2011, 129.
15 The powdered gum no longer stands, having been a casualty of the February 2014 storm.
16 Charles Acton to Ken Hannigan, 18 August 1995.
17 F.W. Burbidge in *The Gardeners' Chronicle*, 17 June 1893.
18 Heavener 1993, 103.
19 *Ibid.*, 103.
20 Liam Price (1945–67, vol. 7) writes that the name Kilma-curra 'probably commemorates St Mochorog'. He unravels the conundrum of the variants of the spelling of Kilma-curra (Kilmacurragh), attributing the form in '-curragh' to Petty's surveyors working for landowners in the seventeenth century, who were accustomed to the word 'curragh', a term often used in maps for marshy places. Though inappropriate for an upland estate such as Kilmacurragh, this form is now the one most frequently used.
21 O'Riain 2011, 479.
22 O'Hanlon 1873.
23 The cell is mentioned in the Life of St Kevin (*Vita Sancti Coemgeni*) in Plummer 1910, vol. 1, 257.
24 Ken Hannigan, 'The Barndarrig Band', *Journal of the Wicklow History Society* 2 (1) (July 1995).
25 Loeber 1994, 274.
26 Cullen 1994, 462.
27 Loeber 1994, 274ff.
28 Hannigan 1994, 794.
29 McCracken 1971.
30 Loeber 1994, 289.
31 Moody and Martin 1967, 190.
32 Turtle Bunbury, 'Acton of Kilmacurragh', author's typescript.
33 *Ibid.*
34 Janet Acton (1824–1906), family archivist, the Kilmacurragh Book, Acton family archive. Courtesy of the Library, National Botanic Gardens, Dublin.
35 Hannigan 1994.
36 The Kilmacurragh Book—the Acton family archive—by Janet Acton (1824–1906) is quoted by kind permission of the Library of the National Botanic Gardens.
37 Pine 2010, 24.
38 *Ibid.*, 20.
39 Letter to the *Irish Times*, 5 May 1999.
40 Pine 2010, 20.
41 *Ibid.*, 10.
42 Money to pay for wars had been raised under this Act, which paid creditors with land forfeited by the 1641 rebels. These and other creditors had mostly resold their property interests to local landowners, who wanted these recent property transfers reconfirmed by an overriding Act for the avoidance of doubt.

43 Pine 2010, 171.
44 RBP, 'Charles Acton, FRIAM, Appreciation', *Irish Times*, 5 May 1999.
45 Pine 1958: 'Thomas Acton, of Bog Hall, Ballygannonbeg and Kilcandra, Co Wicklow (part of the lands of Kilmacurragh), mentioned in Hearth Roll of 1669 as having one hearth in Kilcandra. Will dated 1645 …'. He had a son Thomas, of Bog Hall, and he too had a son Thomas (1671–1750)—presumed the third generation of Actons in Ireland—who began building the house of Kilmacurragh in 1697, aged 26 years, and obtained from Richard, Viscount Rosse, leases for lives renewable for ever of lands in County Wicklow by deeds dated 1716.
46 Queen Anne reigned from William's death in 1702 until 1714.
47 Craig 1976.
48 Peill and the Knight of Glin 2007.
49 Ref. 21 F71, Acton Estate maps, Co. Wicklow, 1698–1829, National Library of Ireland, map section.
50 Pearson 2012.
51 Loeber 1994, 275.
52 Coincidentally, Sir William Robinson was a member of the Irish parliament for County Wicklow from 1695 to 1699, during which time the house was started. While this fact may tempt one to give extra credence to his authorship of the design of the mansion, such an inference may be incorrect. He was credited with transforming Dublin into a major European capital. He was responsible for the design and execution of the Royal Hospital, Kilmainham, Dublin, which established 'standards of monumental classicism', and had a huge influence over his architect successors in Ireland.
53 Craig 1976, 64.
54 Bence-Jones 1988, 41.
55 Charles Acton entry in *Burke's landed gentry* (Pine 1958).
56 Ainsworth report on the Acton papers, National Library, Dublin.
57 Bence-Jones 1988, 41.
58 Lyons 1990.
59 Craig 1976, 64.
60 Peill and the Knight of Glin 2007.
61 Lyons 1990.
62 An almost identical, beautifully preserved staircase in oak is in the Tailors' Hall, Dublin.
63 Wells House, Ballyedmond, Gorey, Co. Wexford, built some years before Kilmacurragh (1664), has similarly positioned fireplaces.
64 Lyons 1990, 9.
65 An extract from a photocopied letter from the Department of Lands, National Parks and Monuments Branch, dated 15 June 1990, included in Lyons 1990.
66 Ainsworth report on the Acton papers, National Library, Dublin.
67 Paul Ferguson, Librarian, Map Library, Trinity College, Dublin.
68 David Griffin, Director, Irish Architectural Archive, Merrion Square, Dublin.
69 Rutherford 1992.
70 Toksvig 1935, 27.
71 Hooker 1849–51.
72 Well's House outside Wexford town, roughly the same size as the Kilmacurragh mansion, was built in 1664. Privately owned and run as a commercial business, it offers tours which provide an interesting reference for all contemporary houses.
73 William of Orange (1650–1702), popularly known as 'King Billy' in Ireland, had introduced his passion for Dutch garden design to England on his accession to the throne (1689); it also became fashionable in Ireland among the Ascendancy landowners.
74 Named after William Robinson (1883–1934), author of *The English flower garden, and home grounds* (London, 1901).
75 F.W.B. (Frederick William Burbidge), *The Gardeners' Chronicle*, 17 June 1893.
76 Bunbury, 'Acton of Kilmacurragh', author's typescript.
77 McCracken 1971.
78 Pine 2010, 23.
79 RDS website.
80 Not only did he publish their names and incomes but he also demanded a tax on all incomes moved abroad, something which was responsible for the economic stress prevailing at the time.
81 Reid 2006.
82 On his appointment (he) had to enter into recognizance to the crown of £1,000 before the barons of exchequer': Donnelly 1994, 868–9.
83 Pine 2010, 24.
84 Bunbury [n.d.].
85 Carey 2009, pp 200, 201.
86 *Ibid*.
87 McCracken 1971.
88 Pearson 2012.
89 Meenan and Clarke 1981.
90 Dr Colin Kelleher, NBG, Glasnevin.
91 Janet Acton, in the Kilmacurragh Book.
92 General stated meeting of the Dublin Society at their Repository in Hawkins Street, on Thursday 4 June 1807.
93 Meenan and Clarke 1981, 186.
94 The exhibits and the story-boards at the gaol were based on the research of historian Joan Kavanagh on behalf of Wicklow County Council. Her primary sources included the 1798 Rebellion Papers (National Archives, Dublin),

the Wicklow Gaol Registers and the Inspector General's Report (placed on a statutory basis since 1823). She collaborated with author Ruan O'Donnell on aspects relating to the transportation of prisoners to Australia, the subject of her current research.

95 Cullen 1994, 487.

96 The Kilmacurragh Book, courtesy of the Library, NBG, Glasnevin.

97 Carey 2009, 225, citing O'Donnell 1988.

98 O'Donnell 1994, 349.

99 *Ibid.*, 372.

100 'Aspects of Wicklow Gaol', Second-year Junior Certificate School Programme Students, Abbey Community College, Wicklow (2007), p. 13.

101 Deirdre Lindsay, St Mary's College, Derry, in her article on the Rebellion Papers (*History Ireland*, (summer 1998), urges cautious use of the archive, 'not least because of the fortuitous means by which the material has come to survive to this day'.

102 'Aspects of Wicklow Gaol', Second-year Junior Certificate School Programme Students, Abbey Community College, Wicklow (2007), 80.

103 The new Horticultural Society in London, founded in 1804, sent out plant-hunters such as David Douglas and Karl Theodor Hartweg (both of whom brought back many magnificent conifers) to the American western coast and Mexico.

104 O'Brien 2011, 331.

105 Veitch 1906, 9–10.

106 Shephard 2003, 78.

107 F.W. Burbidge, British explorer and curator of the Botanic Gardens at Trinity College, Dublin, in *The Gardeners' Chronicle*, 17 June 1893.

108 Shephard 2003, 115, 116.

109 *Ibid.*, 124, 125.

110 *Ibid.*

111 Veitch 1900.

112 Shephard 2003, 151. The Wikipedia entry for William Lobb was also a rich source of reference for this chapter.

113 Baillie 1898.

114 Hannigan 1994, 794: '. . . as late as 1901 in the disposition tenants in Dunganstown, where in 15 out of the 87 townlands Protestants amounted to 50% or more of the population while 45 of the townlands were 100 per cent Roman Catholic'.

115 *Ibid.*, 794, footnote 20, p. 820.

116 Reid 2006.

117 Charles Acton referred to this road as the eighteenth-century coach road from Dublin to Wexford. He claims that another section of it was believed to be in Carrickmines.

118 Clarke 1969.

119 Carey 2009, 85.

120 Pine 2010, 47.

121 John Claudius Loudon (1783–1843), a Scottish botanist and garden magazine editor and author of many botanical encyclopaedias.

122 Ninian Niven (1799–1879), a Glaswegian, curator of the Botanic Gardens, Glasnevin (1834–8), in his correspondence with Loudon.

123 This distinction was pointed out to me by Richard Pine.

124 The IUCN (International Union for the Conservation of Nature) Red List of Threatened Species is the world's main authority on the conservation status of species. (From Wikipedia.)

125 Published by the International Union for the Conservation of Nature and Natural Resources.

126 The Kilmacurragh Book, courtesy of the Library, NBG, Glasnevin.

127 Pine 2010, 50.

128 I am indebted to O'Cathaoir 1994 and Hannigan 1994 for much of the following information.

129 O'Cathaoir 1994, 503.

130 *Ibid.*

131 Hannigan 1994, 799.

132 The Kilmacurragh Book.

133 O'Cathaoir 1994, 544.

134 Hannigan 1994, 791.

135 *Ibid.*, 801.

136 The NAI, CEN 1901 Wicklow 43–45, in Hannigan 1994, 810.

137 O'Cathaoir 1994, 526.

138 Hooker 1854.

139 Bean and Taylor 1976.

140 Hooker 1854.

141 Acton Snee Ayrton, MP and First Commissioner of Works, was an unpleasant snob who did not appreciate the systematic botany of Sir William Hooker and his son Joseph, or the scientific importance of the Botanic Gardens, Kew. He eventually failed to get re-elected to parliament, while Joseph Hooker was elected president of the Royal Society in 1873 by his appreciative fellow scientists.

142 Today, in the 21st century, Hooker's reference work is kept for consultation in the herbarium library at Kilmacurragh.

143 F.W. Burbidge in the *Gardeners' Chronicle*, 17 June 1893.

144 *Ibid.*

145 Pine 2010, 42.

146 *Ibid.*, 37.

147 Frederick William Burbidge, plant-hunter and curator of the Botanic Gardens at Trinity College (1879–1905); William Jackson Bean (1863–1947), British botanist and

148 Burbidge 1903.

149 Robinson 1901.

150 Pine 2010, 31.

151 *Ibid.*, 50.

152 Printed in the *Gardeners' Chronicle*, 12 September 1908.

153 The family tomb is in the graveyard of St Kevin's Church, though she herself is buried with her brother Thomas in an unmarked grave in the Deer Park in Kilmacurragh.

154 Pine 2010, 40.

155 William Watson, curator of Kew Gardens, London, 1901–22.

156 Malins and Bowe 1980, 128.

157 Janet Acton, the Kilmacurragh Book.

158 F.W. Burbidge in the *Gardeners' Chronicle*, 17 June 1893, p. 10.

159 McCracken 1971, 135.

160 Baillie 1898.

161 Farjon 2008.

162 Robinson (1901) mentions several of these.

163 Robinson 1901, 331.

164 *Ibid.*, 33.

165 Farjon (2008) holds that certain living trees of this variety pre-date the Christian era.

166 *Gardeners' Chronicle*, 17 June 1893, signed 'F.W.B.' (Burbidge).

167 The Arnold Arboretum of Harvard University is the oldest public arboretum in North America.

168 Farjon 2008, 219.

169 Pine 2010, 58.

170 The gardens were then administered by the Dublin Society.

171 R.L. Praeger described Moore as 'one of the most clear-sighted and capable of the pioneers of Irish field botany'.

172 During David Moore's curatorship the great national calamity of the potato blight occurred, and it was characteristic of the man that he initiated an important series of experiments on diseased tubers.

173 O'Brien 2008.

174 F.W.B. in the *Gardeners' Chronicle*, 17 June 1893.

175 Pine 2010, 48.

176 Charles later dropped 'Ball' from his name.

177 Courtesy of the Royal Horticultural Society, London.

178 Pine 2010, 49.

179 O'Brien 2011, 329.

180 Pine 2010, 43: an 1865 letter full of vitriolic abuse, 'crooked decrepit buck tooth Acton . . . etc. etc.', from 'The Head Centre' of the Irish Republican Brotherhood, established in 1858, was dubbed sardonically a 'Curious Valentine' by Thomas. Together with its support organisation, the Fenians, the IRB was responsible for a growing rift between landlords and tenants.

181 Charles Acton in a letter to Eric Joyce, custodian of Kilmacurragh, 28 August 1980.

182 Charles Acton's reply to Jack Whaley in a letter to the *Irish Times*, 14 May 1984.

183 Malins and Bowe 1980.

184 In-house information notice for visitors to Kilmacurragh.

185 Viney 2003, 252: 'The common yew is different from the Irish yew which is a chance mutation in which the branches grow stiffly upright and close together, shaping a form as darkly sculptural as an Italian cypress. It dates from about 1740 when a find was made in County Fermanagh.'

186 His niece Irene (1883–1966) refers to a peach-house in her wild-flower notebook.

187 National Library estate maps and papers 1643–1900, on microfilm. Included are the dates of works carried out.

188 Archive, Kilmacurragh Arboretum.

189 The *Gardeners' Chronicle*, 12 September 1908.

190 Pine 2010, 49: Frederick Moore in a letter to Irene Ball-Acton (12 April 1916).

191 Jack Whaley, *Irish Times*, 16 December 1995.

192 Charles Acton to Ken Hannigan in a letter dated 18 August 1995.

193 Departmental letter to the Georgian Society included in Lyons 1990.

194 Craig 1976, 64.

195 Pine 2010, 78.

196 Pihl 1994, 103, 108, 116.

197 Pine 2010, 98, 99.

198 The Kilmacurragh archive, courtesy of the Library, NBG, Glasnevin, and the OPW.

199 Finlay 2011: Herr Budina was believed to have been detained by the Russians until 1946.

200 Pine 2010, 160, 161.

201 Newspaper cutting, May 1969, the Kilmacurragh Book.

202 Pine 2010, 160, 161. The next five years were crucial in Charles's self-development.

203 *Ibid.*, 164.

204 *The Irish Times*, 9 April 1992.

205 This point was made in a pamphlet on *The place of a national arboretum in the Irish economy* (1963), written by Prof. J. Doyle, emeritus professor of Botany at University College, Dublin.

206 Pine 2010, 164.

207 The *Wicklow People*, 25 March 1983.

208 Craig 1976, 64.

209 *Irish Times*, 29 April 2006.

210 Craig 1976, 50.

211 A photocopied letter from the Department of Lands, National Parks and Monuments Branch, included in Lyons 1990.

212 Dr David Griffin, Director, Irish Architectural Archive, Merrion Square, Dublin, 2013.

213 *Irish Times*, 28 April 1984, Gardening Supplement.

214 Bence-Jones 1988.

215 *Irish Times*, 10 February 1989.

216 See http://en.wikipedia.org/wiki/Development_and_preservation_in_Dublin: 'When in the 1950s a row of large Georgian houses in Kildare Place near Leinster House was demolished to make way for a brick wall an extreme republican Fianna Fáil minister, Kevin Boland, celebrated, saying that they had stood for everything he opposed. He also condemned the leaders of the Irish Georgian Society, established to battle to preserve Georgian buildings and some of whom came from aristocratic backgrounds, as "belted earls".'

217 *Irish Times*, 26 November 1992.

218 *Ibid.*

219 *Ibid.*, 11 March 1994.

220 *Ibid.*, 26 November 1992.

221 *Irish Times*, 20 August 2007.

222 Pearson 2012.

223 Correspondence from the private secretary of Minister Jimmy Deenihan, 24 March 2014. Ref.131651/AHG.